K's Kitchen

Recipes and Recollections from the 1930's and 1940's

by [illegible]

3 Rivers Publishing Co.
Carroll County, Mississippi

Contact us: slvhtexas@yahoo.com
Printed in the United States of America

Table of Contents

K's Kitchen

We called our mother K. Her name was Katie. Lila and Lois called her 'Mama' until Lila was four years old. K and Daddy were teaching her the letters of the alphabet: *radio starts with R; Katie starts with K.* Lila started saying K instead of Mama. K liked it, and as the rest of us came along, that's what we all called her.

Day by day, K gave her life for us in so many ways. She lived a long life, influencing the lives of many children.

> Her children rise up and call her blessed.
>
> Proverbs 31

K's kitchen was the heart of our home. We gathered there three times a day - for breakfast, dinner, and supper - holding hands around the table while we thanked God for our food.

K spent much of her day there, cooking, canning, churning, setting lightbread dough to rise, making something special for dessert, and cleaning up after all of that.

We sat at the kitchen table doing homework, playing Old Maids or Hop-Ching Chinese Checkers, picking out pecans, talking and visiting.

Every Saturday night, K put the big No. 10 washtub next to the warm kitchen stove and filled it with warm water, and we took turns getting our Saturday night bath "whether we needed one or not."

And it's true, I was actually born in the kitchen, but that's a different story.

Stories

K-K-K-Katie 1948

I was 8 years old; Ben was 3. He wanted to swing with me, so I set him across my lap, his legs sticking out behind me. I felt big, like Lila and Lois, helping the little children. Ben held on tight to the swing ropes and squealed with delight as we went flying. We both started singing one of our favorite songs.

K-K-K-Katie! Beautiful Katie!
You're the only g-g-g-girl that I adore!
When the m-moon shines over the cow shed,
I'll be waiting at the k-k-k-kitchen door.

I always thought of K and Daddy when I sang that song. Daddy would be outside in the moonlight singing to K who would be, as always, in the kitchen.

Well, it sounded romantic to me.

Prayers

1933

Two-year-old Lois was saying the blessing; "God is great, God is good, Let us thank Him for our food, and God: Lila stole a funny little doll at Mr. Sides's store." Lila's head jerked up! Her parents no longer had heads bowed and every eye closed; they were staring straight at *her*. K and Daddy talked to three-year-old Lila about "we don't do that," and they took the little doll back to the store.

Most of the time we didn't say memorized prayers; we prayed our own words, whatever was in our heart, but several prayers K taught us are still meaningful to us today.

****

Thank You for the world so sweet,
Thank You for the food we eat,
Thank You for the birds that sing,
Thank You, God, for everything.

****

Now before we work today,
We must not forget to pray to God,
Who kept us through the night
And waked us with the morning light.

Help us, Lord, through all this day
In our work and in our play;
Help us to do the things we should
To be to others kind and good.
For Jesus Sake, Amen.

Canning 1950

"Are you in the bedroom?"

"No."

"Are you in the kitchen?"

"Yes."

"Are you behind the door?"

"No."

We were sitting in a circle in the big, new family room playing "Guess Where I'm Hiding" while shelling purple hull peas, all seven of us children – Lila, Lois, G, Mat, Saralou, Margaret, and Ben – our hands busy with the peas, but our imaginations working on our "Twenty Questions" style game.

"Are you under the table?" G asked.

"No."

I guess my smile and the look in my eye gave me away, because Lois asked, "Could you really hide in this place you're thinking of?"

"No."

That needs to be the first question asked in this game, because if you are only imagining, you could be anywhere.

"Are you in the matchbox?" Mat asked. The matchbox hanging on the wall behind the kitchen stove was one of our favorite I-couldn't-really-hide-there places.

"No."

"Are you on the table?" asked Lila.

"Yes."

"You're in the salt shaker!" Margaret yelled.

"Yes! Now you hide somewhere."

Just then Daddy came in from the car with another bushel of peas. He pulled up his chair and started shelling with us. K came from the kitchen with a big boiler and we all dumped in the peas we had shelled. Her hair damp and her face sweaty from standing over the hot canner on a hot stove, K smiled real big and said, "Oh, Lester, this is wonderful. Look at all this good food we'll have for the winter!"

She hurried back to her hot, hard work in the kitchen, and we went on with our game. Margaret hid in the teapot, Lois hid in the sewing machine drawer, Ben hid under the bed, and the peas got shelled.

When I looked in the kitchen, K was pouring hot peas into quart jars. The pan held just enough hot liquid to come to the top of the peas in each jar. She wiped the top of a jar, put on a jar lid from the little pan of boiling water, and tightened on a jar ring. She was putting the jar down into the steaming water in the big, heavy canner when she looked up and saw me standing there.

"Do you need something?" K asked.

"No, just looking. We shelled lots of peas." I felt good that I could be a part of it. A cuptowel on the table held quart jars of peas. One of them went "Ping!" as it cooled and the jar lid sealed on.

"Run on out and play," K said, "I'll call you when supper's ready," and she went back to her work.

We Own a Farm! 1936

In 1936, Daddy got a $300 bonus from his World War One benefits. He used it as a down payment on a 51 acre farm, good sandy loam, two miles south of Winnsboro, Texas. The family couldn't move onto the farm until January 1st, so Daddy rented a little house nearby.

Daddy and Lila went over to the farm and got peanuts out of the old barn; they took them back to the rent house to roast and eat. Lila said, "Daddy, won't the people be mad if we get peanuts out of their barn?" Daddy said, "Oh, we've bought those peanuts. We bought the farm, and we're going to live there." Lila said, "We own a farm?!!?" Then she ran around screaming, "We own a farm!!! We own a farm!!!" It's a wonderful thing to own your own land.

Of course we had a big garden. For the six years we lived on the Winnsboro farm, what we ate was what we grew. Daddy raised acres of sweet potatoes, walking long rows behind a plow and a mule. He grew sweet corn, field corn, popcorn, peanuts, strawberries, and watermelons. We had a peach orchard, a vineyard of concord grapes, a big pear tree, plum tree, wild plum thicket, possum grapes, hickory nuts, black walnuts, and lots of blackberries down in the pasture liberally sprinkled with chiggers.

Picking berries, K and Daddy each had a bucket; each child had a cup. When their cup was full they emptied it into a bucket. K asked, "Lois, are you putting berries into your cup?" Lois answered, "I'm putting them in a cup with a hole in the back," pointing into her mouth. K laughed, and forever after quoted, "Cup with a hole in the back!"

Lois said, "We helped Daddy plant, hoe, and gather. We helped K feed the chickens, gather the eggs, milk the cows, draw water from the well for the house and for washday, hang out the wash, bring in the clothes, wash the dishes, make the beds, sweep the kitchen, churn the butter..."

Lila said, "They couldn't have made it without us."

K worked long, hard days cooking, canning, and sewing. Daddy worked long days in the fields, the older children working beside him. But the attitude was relaxed. The work was done with a song, a joke, a game, or a contest: "I'll beat you to the end of the row and pick more than you do!" "I can spit watermelon seeds farther than you can."

They lovingly helped the little ones "work" too. We wanted to help because that's what our family was doing. The smallest child could pick up kindling chips into the little basket, or carry in small sticks for the fire, amid much encouragement and praise.

If everybody was peeling pears, K gave the little one a slice of pear on a tin plate and a table knife to chop it with, even though it was more likely to be eaten than added to the preserves.

We all helped peel fruit for preserves. A common joke of the day was, "We'll have to make jelly after you!" if the peelings came off too thick. K *always* made jelly with the peelings, with no mention of how thick we had peeled them. We wanted jelly anyway.

Lois remembers one time, when the big ones were shucking corn, Mat gathered up the corn worms. He made a fence of corn shucks and had a full-time job keeping the worms in it. "Get back in there, Billy!"

K canned hundreds of jars of fruits and vegetables. On our farm in the 1930's, the kitchen had no running water, no kitchen sink, no electricity, no cabinets, no pantry, no shelves for storing all those jars of food. K put them under all the beds. Daddy said, "What we need is a cellar, and not just a little storm cellar, either." He got busy and built a big, wonderful basement. He dug a big hole right next to the house ten feet wide, twenty feet long, and six feet deep. He poured a cement floor, built frames and poured cement walls. The walls extended two feet above ground level. Daddy installed two windows in the south wall; they didn't open, but they let in light. Then he built rows of shelves, like at the library, and K filled them with all her jars of home-canned fruits and vegetables.

On top of the basement, Daddy built a wonderful sleeping porch with windows all around to let the cool breezes blow through in the summertime. When it rained a lot, the creek got out all over the bottoms, and oh my goodness alive, how those frogs did sing! They sang us to sleep and were still at it if we woke up in the night.

Daddy built a nice, big barn that Lois calls a hip-roofed barn; the roof slanted then changed the angle of the slant about halfway down. There were lean-to roofs on the sides, stalls and bins inside, and a wonderful big hay loft where we stored corn, peanuts, and hay, and where the children loved to play. Then he built a sweet potato house with double walls, insulated with sawdust which he got free from the planer mill.

Life on the farm was not all work. Lois and G found two metal rims from wagon wheels. Lois named hers Maude and G named his Bing. G said, "Maude and Bing rolled many happy miles, and we were right there with them. Tin cans, pieces of wood, bottles, and rocks became trucks, tanks, or planes, made roads and bridges, served as mountains and hiding places."

One of my earliest memories: Two little girls with buster brown haircuts sitting on the dirt under a shade tree making frog houses. K called them frog houses. She said a little frog may come hopping along and see our little house, just the right size for a frog, and he might move in and live there. Of course, none ever did, but we had that picture in our mind and to us frog houses is what they were. It's a little bit like making sand castles on the beach. You put your bare foot firmly on the ground and don't let it move while you pat moist dirt on top of it. Keep patting on dirt till you think it is strong enough that it would hold its shape without your foot in there to hold it up. Very slowly and carefully, gradually pull your foot out. There you have that little house where a frog could live!

Lila, Lois, G, and Mat made whole villages of frog houses with roads around them where they drove their woodblock cars. Lois found a broken piece of china with a curve on it that made a smooth track; it was perfect for road building. They scooped up dirt and made dirt-walled corrals for the doodle bugs. Everybody decorated their frog houses with flowers and had contests to see who could build the prettiest one. When I got big enough, they taught me to make frog houses, too.

Popcorn

Daddy was the only farmer we knew who grew his own popcorn. It's real easy to grow; you just have to get hold of some popcorn seed and plant it like regular corn. One important thing: You need to plant the popcorn far away from the sweet corn so they won't cross pollinate.

All through the long hot summer, the popcorn grew. First, little ears set on each stalk. The tassels dropped their pollen onto the corn silk and the popcorn grew inside the ear. The silks dried up and the popcorn ears grew bigger while the corn leaves rustled in the wind. The wind grew cool; stalks and leaves started turning brown.

One fine fall morning Lila, Lois, and Daddy walked out into the popcorn field. Almost all the stalks and leaves had turned brown. The ears of corn were brown and dry. Daddy said, "See how the ears are drooping down? That means they're ready to be cut."

Daddy went down the row with a cane knife, cut each stalk near the ground, and laid the stalks across the row. Lila and Lois came along behind. Lila picked up several stalks, made them into a bundle and held them while Lois wrapped the binders' twine around them and tied a knot. When all the popcorn stalks were cut and bundled, the girls helped Daddy gather six or eight bundles, leaning them together at the top, to make a corn shock. "Now we'll leave the corn in the shock a few days," Daddy said.

Another Saturday morning Lila, Lois, and Daddy went back out to the popcorn field. They carried the stalks with the popcorn ears still on them into the barn. Lila and

Lois climbed up in the loft and Daddy passed the bundles up to them till they had all the corn piled up safe and dry. They would pull off ears of corn later, when they needed them.

One cold windy winter's afternoon, walking out the schoolhouse door, Lois tied her headscarf tighter; Lila buttoned up her coat. They turned their backs to the cold north wind and walked the two miles home from school. After a while they turned onto Stout Road, then onto the little wagon road and up the steep hill. Before they got to the grass driveway they could smell the popcorn popping.

"Popcorn!" said Lila.

"Popcorn balls!" said Lois.

They ran as fast as they could toward K's Kitchen.

Popcorn

½ cup popcorn 2 Tbsp. shortening

K put the popcorn and shortening into a pan with a tight-fitting lid. She shook the pan back and forth on top of the hot stove while the corn popped. Then she poured it out into a bowl, sprinkled on salt, and everybody dug in!

Molasses Popcorn Balls

1 cup molasses ½ cup sugar ½ cup water
1 Tbsp. butter ½ tsp. salt

Butter sides of pan; cook to hard ball stage. Pour over 4 quarts popped corn. (Take the hard kernels out of the popped corn first.) Mix well. Butter hands; shape balls.

Watermelons 1940

G's eyes flew open when he heard the screech of the oven door. "I smell bacon and biscuits!" Mat said beside him. They jumped out of bed. Mat got dressed quickly while G put on his new school clothes. It was the day after Labor Day, G's first day of school. After breakfast, Lila, Lois, and G picked up their new pencils, tablets and school lunches and started out the door. Mat followed them all the way down the wagon road, saying goodbye, then he ran back home to play while G went on to school.

By three o'clock G was real ready to go home. As soon as he and Lila and Lois got to the edge of town, G sat down beside the road, took off his shoes and socks, and stuck them in his pockets.

Two miles was a long, hot walk for a little boy. As they came walking up the hill on the little wagon road, G heard Mat's eager voice calling, "G! Hey, G! Come look what we got for you!" Mat came running out to meet his brother and pulled him toward the shade tree over by the well where two watermelons were cooling in the wash tub. Mat was jumping up and down. "I got 'em for you," he said. "I carried 'em both from the watermelon patch all the way up here so they'd be ready soon as you got home."

G looked at his three-year-old brother. "You couldn't! You're not big enough to carry even one." But Daddy said, "Yes he did! Mat took a tow sack and put two melons in it; he carried and dragged them all the way to the well so he could welcome his big brother home."

The cool, juicy watermelons sure did taste good. And G felt proud his little brother cared that much.

"K, Can I Have a Carrot?" 1941

A favorite afternoon snack was a piece of cornbread or a biscuit with a radish, onion, or carrot fresh from the garden. We could pull them ourselves, but we had to ask permission first.

K was taking her afternoon break sitting in her rocking chair out in the shade of the mulberry tree with her feet up, reading her who-dun-it. Lila ran across the yard to K's side asking, "K, can I have a carrot?"

"Yes, dear, bring me one." Lila ran to the garden.

Lois ran to K. "K, can I have a carrot?"

"Yes, dear, bring me one." Lois ran to the garden.

G ran over. "K, can I have a carrot?"

"Yes, dear, bring me one." G ran to the garden.

Little Saralou toddled along behind. "K...me...'runt?"

Mat piped up, "Yes, dear, you're a little runt."

But K smiled and said, "Yes, dear, you can have a carrot, and you too, Mat. Bring me one."

The big girls felt around the tops of the carrots in the garden dirt till they found one big enough to pull. "Here, Saralou, pull this one." Everybody got two. We washed the dirt off in the rain barrel. The weather was warm enough that a little rain barrel splashing felt good, so we splashed each other some.

We ran to give K her five carrots. She took them and her book and headed toward the kitchen, but all us children ran to play, eating our carrots Bugs Bunny style with the green leaves still on.

"Eh? What's up, Doc?"

Homegrown Molasses

K carried a hot pan of biscuits straight from the oven to the table and put one on each person's plate. Lila and Lois were helping me get my greyhoss ready. Lila put a spoonful of butter on my plate and Lois poured on a generous dollop of sorghum molasses then I stirred it up real good. All the children made greyhoss and sopped it up with the hot biscuits.

Lois said, "We watched them make this molasses yesterday out at the syrup mill." I wished I could have gone, but I was too little. Even G and Mat weren't big enough to go spend a whole day at the syrup mill where the men were working.

Daddy had grown five acres of sugar cane in a wet field down across the creek, to make ribbon cane syrup with. Sorghum likes the upland, same as corn, and Daddy had planted a big patch of that, too. It made the good sorghum molasses that we were eating. Daddy always cut the cane and hauled it to the syrup mill. This time he said Lila and Lois could go with him. They spent the whole day watching the men make the molasses.

"We brought nine buckets of syrup home," Lois said, "plus the men got to keep some as their pay for making it."

"They earned it," Daddy said. "Making syrup is hard work." Lila and Lois told us how they did it.

The men fed the ends of the sorghum cane stalks into some big rollers that mashed the sweet juice out. They had a mule walking around and around in a circle to keep the rollers going. The juice ran down into a bucket. Every time a bucket got full they poured the juice into the big metal vat, or pan, about five feet wide, twelve feet long, and six inches deep. The men kept putting more wood on the fire under the pan while the juice bubbled and steam came up thick and heavy. They had long-handled wooden things to push the syrup from one side to the other and across some wooden bars as the syrup got thicker and thicker. As the syrup boiled, a scum formed on the top. The men skimmed it off with long-handled strainers and threw it over into a big hole they called the skimming hole.

Daddy laughed, "That reminds me of Papa and Cousin Buddy making sorghum molasses in Georgia." We all sat back and listened as he told us the story:

Papa and Buddy enjoyed having a loafer come around sometimes; they got a skimmin' hole ready for him. They dug a round hole about two feet across. As the syrup cooked and the scum formed on top of it, they skimmed it off with strainers fixed to a stick about the size of an umbrella handle, then they slung it into the skimmin' hole. When they had a hole filled with the filthy, sticky mess, they covered it with cane chews and slouched a shovel of ashes and charred coals on top so no one could tell the skimmin' hole was there. Then they tried to trick somebody into stepping into it.

Bob arrived at night. Buddy began to tell Bob about a crow's nest in the pin oak tree overhead. Bob asked, "What would a crow do with a nest in September?"

Buddy said, "That makes no difference; the nest is up there! Stand right over here and I'll show it to you."

Bob came closer, staring into the inky overhead.

Buddy said, "Right over this way a little further, Bob."

Bob stepped just a little farther, and fell right into the skimmin' hole! When he got up he was a drippy, sticky mess. Everybody laughed. Bob was mad at first, but the next day he told Buddy, "Let's get Allen next."

By the time Allen showed up, they had two holes ready. He could see the hole which was in current use, and he was careful to avoid it. By taking plenty of distance to be sure not to get into it, he stepped into one of the blind holes. Then, of all things, in an effort to get away from the filthy mess-pot as far as possible, he stepped wide and into the *other* blind skimmin' hole. That set the headlines for community laughs and fun for a long time!

There came a night when the prank backfired. Buddy's father, Mr. Henry McNeely, was our landlord; we were sharecroppers on his land. That night Mr. McNeely, Mamma, and Cousin Mollie came to visit the syrup mill. Papa and Buddy were thrilled with their visitors, but they were also busy in their work. Well, a little too busy at the critical moment when old Mr. McNeely stumbled into the skimmin' hole. He fell, rolled sidewise, and looked up at his son and his renter. He shook his fist at them quivering with anger, and growled, "Now laugh!"

"Did you laugh?" we asked.

"No! Everybody apologized. Mamma and Mollie hurried to get him some clean clothes. Nobody laughed," Daddy said, but the beginning of a laugh was playing around the corners of his mouth.

"You're laughing now," Lila said.

At that, Daddy burst out laughing and we all laughed with him. "You're right! We laughed that night after Mr. McNeely left, and we've been laughing about it ever since!"

Wild and Free

The day was hot and sultry without a breath of air, and the wood-burning stove heated the kitchen like a furnace. K longed for a cool breeze, wished she could take a break under the shade tree, but she had to finish this last canner load of green beans; so she set that determined look on her face and kept her hands and feet moving, set her mind to thinking of food for the winter and of the growing store of quart jars on the basement shelves.

The children playing in the dirt under the mulberry tree looked up when we felt a faint stirring of a breeze. Leaves fluttered overhead, little white clouds hurried across the sky. A little whirlwind chased across the field, stirring up dust. The air felt different. A fresh cool wind blew across the yard, and the little calves in the pasture started jumping around! We stood up and ran in fresh excitement around the yard, into the wind.

K heard our squealing as she took the last jar from the canner, felt a cool wind blow through the hot room. She stood in the back door for a minute holding the screen door wide open, then she stepped into the back yard and turned slowly around in a circle, eyes closed and arms outstretched, relishing the cool air. Suddenly she ran into the wind with us, her arms stretched wide.

Dark clouds scuttled across the sky, trees bent, swooped, and danced, and up-side-down shirts on the clothesline flapped their arms. Birds soared and dived singing wild, sweet songs. If we'd had some wild horses they would have been running along the crest of the hill with manes and tails flying, but since we didn't, it was just us, running into the wind. Wild and free!

Aunt Lucile

Aunt Lucile taught school in the big city of Paris, Texas. We knew school teachers made good money cause Aunt Lucile always had gum in her purse. She always had celery when we visited. She even had waxed paper.

Aunt Lucile and Aunt Sabie, K's sisters, lived on the fourth floor of the Belford Apartments just across from Bywaters Park. The apartments had an elevator with an elevator operator! G and Mat stayed a week with them in the summertime. G said, "Have you ever been up at the top of a four story building? The cars looked like little ants crawling around down there."

Then it was the girls' turn to spend a week. Every day Lila and Lois went to the cowboy picture-show then they went to Uncle Walter's drug store and got a malted milk or a milk shake. Every day! And each day they went to help Aunt Sabie take her little dog, Scooter, for a walk in the park, so they called it Scooter's Park.

When Aunt Sabie started nursing school at the Lamar County Sanatorium, she moved into the student's quarters upstairs. Lila saw her one time with some other students sitting on their upstairs windowsill with their legs out the window, their feet on the roof which covered the outdoor patio below. Lila thought, "Matron won't like that." Matron was the lady in charge. Everybody said, "Yes, Matron." "No, Matron."

Every summer Aunt Lucile spent most of the month of June at our house at Winnsboro, helping with the canning and sewing. We children stood on top of our hill, watching for her. When we saw her car coming down Stout Road and turning onto the wagon road, we started jumping up and down. "She's here! She's here!" and we ran toward the driveway. K came running out the door to join in the hugs and greetings, her whole face and eyes smiling.

"I need some big strong boys to carry in these bags!" Aunt Lucile said, so G and Mat took care of that. She handed Lila and Lois each a box of material and sewing things that she had bought at the fabric stores in Paris. She always watched the sales; when they put the cloth on special, she bought up a bunch of it. I lifted my little arms saying, "Pick me up!" Aunt Lucile handed K the pieces of material she had draped over her arm and carried me inside, saying, "Look how big you're growing!"

Soon they had material spread out on the kitchen table pinning on patterns and cutting out school dresses for Lila and Lois, teacher dresses for Lucile, a dress or two for K, and shirts for Daddy and the boys. Larger scraps made play clothes for the smaller children; little scraps went into the quilting bag for K to work on through the winter.

Canning season was a time for rejoicing. As each fruit and vegetable came ripe, we shelled and peeled by the bushel and put up quart jars by the dozens. Canning started first thing after breakfast, and the stove stayed hot all morning. By afternoon it was just too hot to can, so they pulled out the old Singer treadle sewing machine and stayed busy sewing.

One bright summer day, Aunt Lucile led a parade of us pickers to the peach orchard; K walked beside her, talking and laughing, carrying several bushel baskets. We ate the over-ripes, juice running down our chins, as we filled the baskets with peaches and carried them to the house.

We were allowed to eat as we peeled, but that day everybody just kept eating. After a while Aunt Lucile reached in her school-teacher purse and passed around sticks of Juicy Fruit gum. "Oh boy! Chewing gum!" After that, the peaches mostly made it to the canner.

Aunt Lucile offered Daddy a piece of gum, too, but he said with a little grin, "No thanks, it would get in my way."

In the evenings, sitting on the big porch swing hanging from a limb of the chinaberry tree, Aunt Lucile brushed her hair while she told us stories, many of them from her first-grade readers. She had a really good deep, gruff Papa Bear's voice, "Somebody's been eating my porridge!" and the little squeaky Baby Bear's voice, "Somebody's been eating my porridge, too, and they ate it all up!"

She told us about one of her little first-grade boys who simply would not behave. She said, "I was just about to give him a paddling, when I looked down and saw his little bare feet. I thought, *those little feet have a long way to go.* So I just talked to him one more time."

When Aunt Lucile went back to Paris, she took jars of fruits and vegetables home with her, and some fresh produce, too, whatever was in season.

One time when Aunt Lucile came to visit, she brought her new friend to meet us. He was soon to become our Uncle Victor. We liked him. He brought us a whole candy bar each! Daddy performed their wedding at Aunt Lucile's apartment in Paris in the fall of 1942. Margaret was a little baby. They told me to throw the rice, but I wanted to eat it instead. Aunt Lucile and Uncle Victor moved to a big, wonderful house on Bonham Street, where we had many memorable visits through the years.

Parched Peanuts

The piles of corn stalks and dry peanut plants gave off an earthy, musty smell as we climbed into the barn loft and started picking peanuts from the plants. We rubbed the dirt off between the palms of our hands, and put the nuts in the pan. It was a cold, drizzly, rainy day, and a bunch of active children cooped up in the house had been a little too much for everybody. K said, "Run out to the barn and pick off a pan full of peanuts and we'll parch them. It will be a surprise for Daddy when he gets home."

Oh, Boy! Parched Peanuts!

We had the pan almost full when Daddy walked into the barn and started milking the cows. Lois whispered, "Shhh... Don't let Daddy hear us. It's a surprise." We worked quietly with quiet giggles then slipped down from the loft. We got to the barn door just as Daddy stepped out of the cow stall. G hid the pan of peanuts behind his back, but little Saralou blurted out, "It's a surprise; it's parched peanuts!" Everybody laughed and went on inside.

The fire in the wood-burning stove had burned down pretty good. Daddy said the temperature should be just right. "We don't want the stove so hot it burns the peanuts," he explained as he set the pan in the oven.

We let them bake 30 minutes or so before we started testing to see if they were done. K used a folded cuptowel to pull out the pan. We each got one or two peanuts. You break open the shell and rub the nut with your fingers. If the little skin rubs off easily, they're done. Of course the first ones weren't, but we got to eat them half-cooked, then after a while we tried another one.

Mat started singing, "Found a peanut, found a peanut, found a peanut just now; I just now found a peanut, found a peanut just now."

It's one of those songs that goes on and on forever and drives you crazy if you aren't the one singing it, so we all started singing it. "Broke it open, broke it open, broke it open just now..." "Found it rotten...."

The next time K pulled out the peanuts to let us test them, they were done and everybody dug in. Boy Howdy! We had some good eating!

Mat started in again, "Ate it anyhow, ate it anyhow... Got sick... Called the doctor... Died anyhow... Went to heaven, went to heaven, went to heaven just now...." The tune is like "Oh, My Darling, Clementine" in case you want to sing with us. Or you could just send us out to the barn loft.

We children spent many hours in the barn loft, picking off peanuts, shucking corn, or just playing around. We threw the empty peanut vines down to feed the milk cows and the plow mule. Daddy planted lots of peanuts; he wanted his children to have some real treats.

Uncle Bill always gave us a sack full of pecans for Christmas. Our present to him was a sack full of peanuts. We spent a long time in the barn loft taking extra care to get off every bit of dirt and to pick only the best nuts.

Parched Peanuts - Bake peanuts in the shell at 300 degrees, for 45 minutes or more, until the thin skin on the shelled nut rubs off easily and the nut tastes done. Just keep on testing and tasting.

Mr. Tom Kay's Pomegranates 1944

Daddy was the pastor of the Baptist Church in Yantis. Mr. Tom Kay led the music. When he led the song, he didn't wave his arm around. He stood with his right arm straight down by his side and patted his hand up and down as he patted his foot in time with the music.

Down at the Cross where my Savior Died,
Down where for Cleansing from Sin I Cried,
There to my Heart was the Blood applied;
Glory to His Name!

No polished, professional performance here, just honest, heartfelt, praise to our Creator and Savior. Tom Kay was a dear old man and we loved him dearly.

One Sunday, somebody mentioned pomegranates, and K let it be known how much she liked them. Mr. Kay said, "I have bushels of them all getting ripe at once. They're falling on the ground and rotting. Come get all you want."

Far be it from us to let good food go to waste, especially pomegranates. We all piled into the car and drove the two miles out in the country to Mr. Kay's house. He had a long hedge of pomegranate bushes, twelve feet tall and loaded with fruit. What riches! We picked a bushel basket full and carried them home with us, where we could have all we wanted, besides the ones we ate right there in the yard while Daddy and Mr. Kay stood around talking. We pulled off pieces of the tough, leathery peel and dug out sections of the little hard seeds each covered with a sack of sweet-tart red juice. Chomp down on a mouthful and feel the flavor explode on your tongue!

The New January 1945

Ben was born January 3rd, two days after the New Year. When he was three or four years old, Ben said, "When we get the New January, I'll get my birthday." We started quoting that on him, and once our family starts quoting something, you never live it down.

We had just moved to Union. Lila and Lois helped K walk up the little hill to the house, and she sat down while everybody else carried in the boxes. In just a few days, Daddy took K to the hospital in Winnsboro. Soon they came back, bringing along a baby brother for us named Ben. G and Mat were fishing in the pond when Daddy's car drove up to the house. "Must be K and the baby," they said, and kept on fishing. Saralou and Margaret came bouncing down the trail yelling and carrying on about, "K and the baby are home! Come see the baby!" The boys' response: "Be quiet, you'll scare the fish."

Lois was in the 9th grade, Lila in the 10th. They took two weeks off school to help take care of us. In those days a lady stayed in bed for ten days after a new baby came. Aunt Lucile would have come to help if it had been summer, but Lila and Lois did just fine. K was in bed with the baby, and she told them what to do, and when and how to do it, just like she always did when they helped around the house. They opened jars of fruits and vegetables and cooked our usual bacon, ham, and sausage, with biscuits, and Daddy made the gravy. They washed the dishes and swept the floors. As always, they helped the little ones and wiped our noses. And we were all glad to have a new little brother. Lila said, "Ben was a blessing to all of us."

Warm Feet

Outside, the cold wind moaned and whistled around the house corners and rattled the windows like it was trying to get in; and if the wind couldn't, well the cold did. The floorboards felt like ice under our cold feet. Margaret and I shivered as Lila and Lois helped us into our sleeping clothes. We ran into the other room, where Daddy had a blazing fire going in the big wood-burning stove; we jumped into his lap, Margaret on one side, me on the other. "Sing us a song," I begged, "That sad one, about the boy that didn't get to go home."

So Daddy sang "When the Work's All Done This Fall." The boy kept saying he was going home to see his mother, but he kept putting it off until it was too late. K came in and put some bricks to warm on the stove. I felt glad we didn't have to go anywhere to see our mother, glad our whole family could be at home and safe together.

Daddy reached for the jar of Vicks Vaporub. First he coated Margaret's feet, and then his tough, strong hands rubbed the menthol salve on mine. We held our feet out toward the stove, laughing while our feet got toasty warm and the pungent Vicks smell filled the room, which felt much warmer now. K wrapped each hot brick in a cuptowel and carried some to the boys' room, then some to the girls' room. Daddy carried Margaret, then me, to bed and slipped us under the covers. And there, just where my feet would naturally be, I felt the warm brick wrapped in K's cuptowel. Lila, Lois, and Margaret had warm bricks at their feet, too. Soon we fell asleep with warm feet and warm hearts, knowing we were loved.

When the Work's All Done This Fall

A group of jolly cowboys discussing plans at ease,
Said one, I'll tell you something, if you will listen, please.
Once I had a home, boys, and a good one you all know;
You know I haven't seen it, since a long, long time ago.

Now when I left my home, boys my Mother for me cried;
She begged me not to go boys for me she would have died.
I'm going back to Dixie once more to see 'em all;
I am going home, boys when the work's all done this fall.

When the roundup days are over 'n the shipping all is done,
I'm going straight on home boys, before my money's gone.
I have changed my ways, boys, no more will I fall;
I am going home, boys, when the work's all done this fall.

That very night the cowboy went out to stand his guard;
The lightening, it was flashing, and storming very hard.
The cattle, they got frightened 'n rushed in wild stampede
The cowboy tried to turn them while riding at full speed.

While riding in the darkness, alone he did shout;
He did his best to head them and turn the herd about.
His saddle horse did stumble and on him it did fall.
He'll not see his mother when the work's all done this fall.

They buried him at sunrise, no tombstone at his head,
With nothing but a sign-board, and this is what it said:
Poor Charlie died at daybreak; he died from an awful fall;
He won't see his mother when the work's all done this fall.

Measles 1947

I could hear them in the kitchen, talking, laughing, chairs scraping up to the table as they all sat down in their usual places, holding hands around the table while Daddy said the blessing. Only my chair would be empty. Right there between Margaret and Mat, I should have been saying, "Pass the chicken, please," and sticking my fork into a drumstick while Mat and Margaret argued over who got the pulley bone. In fact, I heard their voices raised, then Daddy's quick "Here, Here!" which meant "enough of that!" and they settled down, and everything got quiet as they all started eating.

I was alone in the front room, lying on the couch with a quilt and a pillow, covered with itchy red spots. That one right there on my stomach really began to itch. I had to grit my teeth, and keep telling myself, "Don't scratch! Don't scratch!" because I didn't want my measles spots to get infected and leave scars. I looked around the room. Daddy had nailed quilts over the windows because bright sunlight could damage my eyes. Some people said you could go blind from the measles. The room felt empty. All the furniture was there; it was the people who were missing.

Just then the door opened, and I turned my head away because the light from the other room hurt my eyes. The door closed quickly as K came into the room with a plate of food for me. She had purple hull peas, mashed potatoes and gravy, and a chicken leg; exactly what I would have chosen if I had been at the table with the others.

I sat up on the couch, my legs still covered with the quilt, and K pulled up a chair beside me. "How are you feeling?" she asked, gently touching her hand to my forehead. I didn't have any fever.

"I'm fine," I answered, but a lump rose in my throat because what I really felt was lonesome. Even in the dim light, she could see the tears in my eyes.

"It won't be much longer," she said. "It's been nine days, counting today, and measles usually last only two weeks." *That leaves five more days,* I thought, but I didn't want to complain. Just then a spot on my arm really started itching, and I almost scratched it, but instead I put my hand on it and squeezed.

"Let me look," K said, and I moved my hand. "It looks like it's getting better," she said. "They always itch more when they start getting well." I hoped that was true.

"I wish I could be out there with the others," I whispered, "but I don't want to give them my germs."

"They're thinking about you." K reached in her apron pocket and pulled out a small envelope. Margaret had written me a note that said "I love you" with a red heart drawn around it. Mat sent me a Bluejay feather he found, and Ben put in a small red and brown rock. It felt good to get something from them, but somehow it made me miss them even more. A few tears spilled out of my eyes.

"I don't have anything to send them back." I wanted to send myself. I wanted to run out there and get in the middle of that rambunctious, rowdy bunch and be a part of my family again. I looked through my things, but anything I sent them would have my germs on it.

"That's okay. You rest and get well and you'll be back with them soon." We sat there together as I ate a few bites. I really wasn't very hungry. K looked around the room and said, "Lila and Lois had the measles when we lived at Winnsboro. Daddy tacked quilts over the windows for them just like he did for you here."

In a minute we heard the chairs scraping back from the table then the talk and laughter went out the back door. K stood up. "I guess I better go clean up the kitchen. I'll be back in a little while to see if you're through with your plate. You need to eat your food so you can get well and strong again."

I took a bite and slowly chewed and swallowed. Then I smiled, remembering something I had said when I was little, and K had quoted it to me ever since. I had just started first grade and felt so big and so proud of the new word I had learned. So I quoted it now to K. "Us school girls have got to watch our nutrition." That must have been just what she needed to hear, because I saw K smile as she headed back toward the kitchen.

Ben's School Lunch 1948

K hurried to fix everybody's school lunch: sausage and biscuit, baked sweet potato, a jar of milk. Everybody grabbed their lunch and headed out the door. Daddy went to Meadowview School, G to Greenville High. Lila and Lois caught the Trailways bus to the college in Commerce. Mat, Saralou, and Margaret walked two miles to Center Point, a two-room country school. That left only Ben home with K. Ben needed a lunch, too! So K fixed him one. He took it outside and ate it. After that, K packed Ben's lunch when she did ours. Every morning he walked with us almost to the big road, sat down under a shade tree, and ate his lunch; then he took the sack back inside to K's kitchen.

Jello on the Roof 1949

It was a beautiful January with lots of ice and snow. Ice covered everything. Every blade of grass had a coating of ice, every branch, every little twig on the trees, coated with ice so thick they looked like trees of glass, and the cold clear sunlight glittered from a wonderland of cold glass trees.

Lila and Lois were in college! They went to East Texas State Teachers' College, and we had just moved to a little house in the big town of Commerce, Texas. We called it The Doll House because it was way too little for us. We four girls slept in a little attic room with a slanted roof so low that the only place we could stand up straight was right in the middle of the room. The two double beds and a dresser filled the floor space, leaving narrow walkways. Opposite the stairs, a window opened onto the roof.

Lila came up the stairs with a bowl of something in her hands. "What's that?" I asked as I ran to see. It was Jello, freshly made, still warm. We had eaten some at Aunt Lucile's house, but we had never made any because we didn't have a refrigerator.

"Let's set this outside the window on the roof and see what happens," Lila said. I opened the window for her. She carefully set the bowl down on the little flat place on the roof and closed the window.

Downstairs, Daddy paced from one window to the other. Huge icicles hung all around the eaves of the house; they were so heavy he thought they might damage the roof. "Boys, come outside and help me." Daddy, G and Mat took hoes and broom handles and knocked the icicles down. Margaret and I wanted to go outside and help, but K said we might get hurt, so we watched through the windows as the icicles came crashing and tinkling down.

After dinner Lila came down the stairs carrying the bowl of Jello. It was cold and it jiggled, just like Aunt Lucile's always did, and we each got some for dessert.

Late that afternoon we heard sounds like gunshots from one side of the house, then from the other. "What's that?!!" we asked each other, running to look out the windows. Daddy went outside to see, and we ran to stand behind him at the door. He shooed us back inside saying, "It's the noise of tree branches breaking because the ice is so heavy on them."

Just then we heard a loud "CRACK!!" then the crash of a huge branch breaking off a tree in the neighbor's yard behind us.

K said, "This reminds me of the winter we got Mat. We had just moved to Winnsboro and were living in the little rented house before we moved onto the farm. We had a bad ice storm like this one, and big limbs were breaking off the trees.

"When they told G he had a new baby brother, he put his little bare feet on the cold floor and ran into the other room to see the new baby. We told G, 'His name is John Matthew, after his two grandpas. We will call him whatever part of that you can say,' and little G answered, 'Him name Mat.' "

We sat around talking and reading until nine o'clock when K sent us all off to bed. We lay there listening to the gunshot sounds of branches breaking from the trees until finally we drifted off to sleep.

Snow Cream 1949

The next morning Ben woke everybody up early yelling, "It's snowing! It's snowing!"

Margaret and I jumped up and looked out our window. Sure enough, we saw big, fluffy snowflakes coming down, and it looked like it had been snowing hard most of the night. We got dressed as quick as we could and ran outside. I lifted my face to the sky; it almost made me dizzy, watching the snowflakes swirling through the air.

It was a beautiful day! The snow lay soft and deep on everything, and the ordinary, everyday things had turned into a winter wonderland. The snow crunched under our feet. We threw snowballs at each other and ran and ducked and laughed. G and Mat started chasing each other around the back yard, trying to put snow down each other's back, but I stayed up close to the house.

K came out into the back yard with a big pan and the egg turner. She used the egg turner to scoop up the top few inches of the snow that lay deep on the picnic table. "You're making snow cream!" I yelled, and I ran inside to get a big spoon to help her.

"Take just what's on top," K said. "If we dig too deep we might get dirt from the table." When the pan was full of clean, fluffy snow, we took it in to the kitchen. K beat a couple of eggs until they were light and fluffy and kept beating while I slowly poured a cup of sugar into them. K stirred in a spoonful of vanilla and a little milk. Then we stirred in enough snow to make it thick like ice cream. All of us sat around eating our bowls of snow cream while K told us a story about when she was a little girl.

"Every time it snowed Mama made a big bowl of snow cream," K started.

"Just like we do!" Ben and Margaret said.

"Just like we do," K agreed. "Mama mixed up sugar and eggs and a little milk and vanilla, and put as much snow in to make it thick like ice cream. We loved it. Mama never did serve it out in little bowls, but she held the big bowl in her lap and we all ate from the same bowl."

"From the serving bowl?"

"Yes. Mama never let us put our spoons in the serving bowls at the table and I'm surprised she let us do it with the snow cream. I guess there was a 'togetherness' about it that she enjoyed. I know we did. Of course we had to watch the others to be sure they didn't get more or bigger bites than we did."

"Yeah, just like Mat!" I said, but at the same instant I said it, Margaret was saying, "Yeah, just like Saralou."

"Just like all of us," K said. "We all want to be sure we get our share."

"Is there any more?" Ben asked, and K said, "No," so we ran out to play in the snow.

Snow Cream

1 egg	$\frac{1}{2}$ cup milk	fresh snow
$\frac{1}{2}$ cup sugar	2 tsp. vanilla	

Beat eggs while gradually adding sugar. Stir in milk and vanilla. Stir in enough fresh, clean snow to make it thick like ice cream. Eat right away; does not keep well.

Buttermilk Kiss 1950

"Saralou, can you help me churn the buttermilk?" K called from the kitchen. "I need to start supper."

"OK," I said, but I didn't want to leave the book I was reading. Meg, Jo, Beth, and Amy were starting a club and writing their own newspaper, things I enjoyed doing, too, so I took *Little Women* with me. One hand held the book while the other pumped the dasher up and down. After a long while, I thought I felt lumps of butter in the milk.

"Let me look," K said. Sure enough, it was ready and she spooned the butter into a bowl, rinsed it with a little cold water, and gently mashed the lump of butter with the back of the spoon, working out the water and whey. She let me stir in a little salt and put the soft fresh butter in the butter dish while she poured up the buttermilk into gallon jars.

Just then G and Daddy came in from milking the cow, and K strained the fresh milk through a clean white cup towel into another gallon jar. She took up the warmed-over butterbeans and the fried potatoes and put them on the table with the leftover cornbread and biscuits, then started pouring glasses of fresh, warm milk. Margaret took a big drink and grinned at me through her milk mustache. I shuddered, cause I can't stand the taste of warm milk, fresh from the cow.

"I want buttermilk," I said, and K brought me a glass of it. I took a drink then grinned at Margaret through a big buttermilk mustache.

"Ooooo!" Margaret shuddered. "I can't stand buttermilk!"

"Then we're even," I gloated as I crumbled cornbread into my buttermilk and ate it with a spoon.

"I'll bet you had buttermilk on your mouth that time you kissed me," Margaret said. "Yuck!"

"When did I ever kiss you?" I asked. We really didn't kiss much around our house.

"That time when I was a baby," Margaret answered. "K told us about it."

As we went into the front room, K told the story again about when we went to the hospital to see our brand new baby sister.

All five of K's children had been born at home. When it was almost time for Margaret, Dr. Stewart said, "I want to deliver this one at the hospital."

"Oh, but it is so much cheaper at home," K said.

"I will charge you the same at the hospital as it would be at home," Dr. Stewart said. "It will be so much easier for me because I will have everything I need there."

Daddy took us five children to the hospital to see our new little sister. I was two years old. A little half door separated K and Margaret's room from the hall with a foot or two of open space under the door.

"I heard the children in the hall," K said, "then here came little Saralou, crawling under the door. She ran straight to the bed and kissed her little sister."

"Yuck!" Margaret said. "A buttermilk kiss!"

I chased Margaret around the room with my buttermilk lips puckered up for a kiss. She squealed and ran to hide behind Lois. I took a shortcut across the room to head her off and brushed behind Daddy who was reading a book.

"Good gracious, Child! Settle down!" Daddy said. We settled down. Lila brought a wet washrag for us to wash the milk off our faces.

"Were you really going to call me Meg?" Margaret asked.

"Like in *Little Women*," Lila said.

"We started calling you Meg," Lois remembered.

"But every time they said Meg, I said Nutmeg," K laughed. "It didn't take long for them to quit trying."

"I like my name just like it is," Margaret said.

And I thought, "I do, too."

Ben's Box

Ben had a box big enough that he could sit in it. It was his car, and he drove it very fast with lots of sound effects. Buddin-buddin-buddin.... Beep, beep! Screeeech! Varoom! "I'm going 95 high speed!"

Then Ben's box was a house for a little animal.
"What kind of animal are you?" K asked.
"When I make my little sound you will know."
Cheep! Cheep! The baby chicken wanted bread.
Woof! Woof! The dog wanted a scrap of meat.
Maa-a-a! Maa-a-a! The calf wanted some milk.
Roawr! The tiger scratched inside the box.

Then the box was a filing cabinet, like Daddy's. "What will you keep in your filing cabinet?" K asked.

"Whadda ya suspect, Pigs?!!!!" He never did say what he had been planning to keep in it.

Daddy's Honey 1950

Daddy was good with bees. They didn't sting him. He was gentle, and he wasn't afraid. Bees can smell fear on you the same way stray dogs and wild bulls can. Daddy handled the beehives gently. We stayed away from them. Until one spring day when the bees swarmed.

We had moved from the Doll House to our wonderful big house on Park Street. When I went out the back door that morning, the bees were everywhere; the whole backyard was just *full* of them, swarming around in a huge circle from about waist high as far up as I could see. For some reason I wasn't afraid of them and they paid me no mind. It looked like a snowstorm when I kinda fuzzed out my eyes and imagined each bee to be a big snowflake.

"You children get back in the house," Daddy said as he headed for the shed to get his bee hat, his smoker, and a bee box. We watched out the back door as the bees started gathering on a low branch of a tree. Daddy lit a smoldering fire on the old rags in the smoker, and when it started puffing out smoke he put on his gloves and the bee hat with a veil covering his face. By then the bees had all settled in a big clump on the tree branch. Daddy told us the queen bee had landed there first, and all her worker bees had gathered around her. Their job was to protect the queen and take care of her, so he had to be careful getting them into the bee box, and we could watch from the porch, but we needed to be quiet.

Daddy calmly and quietly walked to the tree branch. He puffed smoke on the bees till they got sleepy. Then he held the bee box under them and, with two more strong puffs of smoke, they just turned loose and fell gently into the box. Daddy made sure he had the queen bee in there with them then he put the lid on the box.

"Now," he said, "I'll set these bees out in the clover field with the other beehives and they can make us some honey!" Daddy had an arrangement with some farmers who grew alfalfa hay and vetch clover for cattle feed. Daddy needed clover for his bees to make honey, and the farmers needed bees to pollinate their crops. They were glad for Daddy to put his beehives in their hay and clover fields.

"Tell your mama I'll be right back. Tell her I'm bringing some honey home." Daddy put the box of bees in the old Buick and drove away.

We ran in the house and told K, "Daddy's taking the bees to the clover! He said he's bringing home some honey!" K started gathering up the dishpan and the butcher knives.

"Saralou and Margaret, run out to the shed and bring in all the quart fruit jars you can find," K said. We brought in armloads and boxes of jars and helped her wash them in hot soapy water. By the time we had everything clean and dry and laid out on the kitchen table, Daddy drove up with five white honey boxes. They looked smaller than the box of bees he had taken.

"These are supers," Daddy explained. "I don't take any honey from the big boxes where the bees live. They eat that honey and feed it to their babies. But after the big box is full, I put a super on top. The honey they put up there is extra, more than they need, and it is for us to eat."

Daddy carried the boxes inside and he and K started cutting honey in the honeycomb from each frame. K and Daddy put honeycomb in some of the jars, but most of the jars they filled with just honey. K put a big piece of comb in a clean white cuptowel and squeezed the honey out, and then twisted the towel to wring out every last drop of honey. She would melt down the honeycomb to make beeswax. Daddy traded it to the bee supply store for starter frames for the bees to make more honey on. We each got a piece of honeycomb full of honey to chew, and it was good! But K soon told us to go outside and play so she and Daddy could get their work done.

When we came in for supper they had jars and jars of honey filling the cabinets. K had cooked hot biscuits for supper and we had all the honey we wanted to eat!

Starlac Nougats

½ cup honey ½ cup peanut butter 1 cup powdered milk

K found this recipe for honey and peanut butter candy on the package of Starlac Dried Milk. Mix equal parts peanut butter and honey. Stir in enough dried milk to make a stiff candy. We made it into little balls and ate them.

Honey can be used instead of sugar in many recipes. For each cup of sugar, substitute half a cup of honey.

Beeswax is good for many things. You can chew beeswax like chewing gum. Keep needles sharp by rubbing the point on beeswax. Pull thread across a block of beeswax for really heavy sewing, like on leather. You might want to tell your nosy brother or sister, "Mind your own beeswax!"

K's Christmas Fruitcake

K made fruitcake only once a year, but it took her most of the year to do it. The first mention of fruitcake usually came in the middle of the hot summertime when, smiling with pride, Daddy cut a big watermelon on the backyard table. Did he choose a round, dark-green Black Diamond or a long striped Georgia Rattlesnake melon? It didn't matter; we all dug in, sweet red juice dripping from chins and elbows.

K put the big tin dishpan in the middle of the table for the rinds. Usually they went to feed the pigs, cows, and chickens, but this time K looked in the dishpan and said, "This rind is nice and thick. I think I'll make watermelon rind preserves today. I've got to have some for the fruitcake."

With a sharp knife K cut the red and green parts off the rind then chopped the white part into little cubes and put them in a big heavy boiler. She sliced lemons into thin rounds then added sugar. K told me, "You add a cup of sugar for each cup of chopped rind," but I don't think she actually measured the rinds. I think she measured with her eye. Then for a long time she stirred and cooked and cooked and stirred, the pan bubbling and boiling, "until it makes preserves."

"How can you tell when it's done?" I asked.

"It's the same as for jelly." She showed me how to watch a drop gather on the edge of the spoon then slowly drip back into the pan. "It's done!"

K put the hot preserves into clean quart jars and sealed the lids on tight. When they cooled, they went on the shelf with the jars of tomatoes, green beans, purple hull peas, peaches, and jelly. But the preserves were special. They were waiting for the Christmas fruitcake.

Summer days passed. Apples and pears, hanging ripe on the trees, became jars of pear preserves, applesauce, and mincemeat. Mincemeat? That's apples, pears, and green tomatoes cooked with cinnamon, nutmeg, cloves, sugar, vinegar, raisins, and lemon.

"The figs are ripe," a neighbor said, "Come pick some for your fig preserves!" I always thought the figs were the best, cooked with the thin-sliced lemon, sitting in jars on the shelf, waiting for the Christmas fruitcake.

Summer turned to autumn, and colored leaves fell from the trees. Something else fell from the trees, too. Walnuts, hickory nuts, and pecans! Daddy and the children took sacks and buckets and found the nuts under the dry, crunchy leaves. Daddy put a flat rock on his lap then with the hammer – Crack! – the nut was open. K held a flatiron with the handle between her knees and used Mat's little toy hammer to crack some nuts, too. We all helped pick the fat nuts from the shells. I tried to be the first to fill my cup and add my share to K's bowlful. The nuts wouldn't have to wait as long as the preserves had. Soon they would be part of the Christmas fruitcake.

A few days after Thanksgiving K said, "Today we'll make the fruitcake!" Out came that big tin dishpan, scrubbed clean. In went sugar, butter, and eggs. Stir it up real good! Sift in flour, cinnamon, nutmeg, cloves. And finally add all those jars of preserves: Fig preserves!

Pear preserves! Mincemeat! And the watermelon rind preserves saved from that hot summer day; finally all are stirred into the fruitcake, along with lots and lots of nuts.

The oven is hot. The nutty-fruity-spicy batter is in the pans. But wait! Now comes the fun part. Before they bake, we need to decorate the cakes with red cherries and pecan halves laid in pretty patterns. K always made brown pecan flowers with red cherry centers.

Finally the cakes were baked; they came warm from the oven. But did we gobble them up right then? No. K wrapped each cake in a clean white cuptowel and hid them away in the back of a cool, dark dresser drawer, waiting.

One week.

Two weeks.

Three weeks.

Christmas day!

K took something wrapped in a white cuptowel from the dresser drawer. At the table she un-wrapped it, and there was a beautiful fruitcake with pecan and cherry flowers on top. K sliced the cake and put it on a plate for Christmas desert. All day we ate apples, oranges, and that wiggledy ribbon candy from our stockings. We ate Christmas dinner with all the trimmings. But what was best of all?

The Christmas Fruitcake!

K's Fruitcake

2 cups sugar
$\frac{3}{4}$ cup shortening
2 eggs
2 cups flour
2 tsp. baking powder
2 tsp. baking soda
3 tsp. cinnamon
2 tsp. allspice
1 tsp. nutmeg
$\frac{1}{2}$ tsp. cloves
1 quart fig preserves
1 quart pear preserves
1 quart watermelon rind preserves
1 quart mincemeat
1 lb dates, chopped
4 cups pecan pieces
1 pound raisins
$\frac{1}{2}$ cup candied orange peel

Cream together shortening, sugar, and eggs. Sift in dry ingredients alternating with preserves. K added flour till the batter was very moist but not runny. Add dates, raisins, pecans, and candied orange peel. Fill greased and floured loaf pans. Decorate with candied cherries and pecan halves. Bake at 300 degrees for one hour, or until toothpick in center comes out clean.

K's Fruitcake Preserves

K made preserves by adding a cup of sugar for each cup of chopped fruit. Add thin slices of lemon. Cook down until the liquid sheets from a metal spoon. Dip a metal spoon and let the liquid drip back into the pan. If it runs off like water, keep cooking and stirring. If it takes a while for a drop to gather and slowly drip, it is probably done. If it starts trying to spin a thread, you've cooked it too long; preserves will be good, but thick like taffy candy. Seal in hot mason jars with Ball lids.

Recipes for candied orange peel and mincemeat, page 65.

Meat

Rooster, Pullet, Fryer, Hen

Daddy had a little game he played with the younger children. He pointed to the forehead, nose, lips, chin, saying, "Rooster, pullet, fryer, hen." Then pointing to the forehead he asked, "What did I say this is?" and the child answered, "Rooster." Pointing to the chin, "And what is this?" "Hen." Pointing to the lips, "And this?" "Fryer." And last, the nose... "And this?" When the child said "Pullet," Daddy gave the nose a gentle tug and both of them laughed. "You said to pull it!"

General Guidelines for Cooking Meat

1. K cooked only as much as we would eat that day.
We had no refrigerator or freezer to store leftovers.
2. We always took a small serving of meat and a big serving of potatoes and gravy. Many meals were cornbread and vegetables with no meat at all.
3. When K's recipe said grease, she usually meant lard which she rendered from hog fat.
5. Bacon grease was good for seasoning vegetables. K poured bacon grease into an old coffee can set on the stove so it would be handy when she needed to use some.
5. We never threw away grease; old lard and grease saved from cooking were used to make lye soap.
6. We cooked what we grew. We had lots of food, but not much money; what grocery money we had went for staples like cornmeal, flour, baking powder and baking soda, salt, sugar, spices, cocoa powder, and drip-grind coffee.
7. K cooked the meat, but she always called Daddy to make the gravy. He was good at it.
8. Meat scraps, bones, and drippings were used as seasoning for vegetables: bacon grease in the Brown Crowder peas, neck bones in collard greens, dried beans or peas cooked on a hambone, ham scraps in the butterbeans, soup bones in the vegetable soup.
9. Old roosters, and hens too old to lay eggs, made Chicken and Dumplings. Young roosters were fried, but the pullets were kept to become laying hens. 
Rooster, pullet, fryer, hen.

Home-grown Meat

Daddy raised a few hogs every year, so we could have some good **sausage, bacon, and ham**. He smeared sugar cure on the hams and shoulders and hung them from the 2-by-4 rafters in the little shed. K and Daddy mixed spices into the ground-up sausage, cooked a little sample, tasted, put more spices, tasted again. We had fun tasting samples! **Spareribs, pork loin, and backbone** were not smoked or cured. K sliced and fried the fresh spareribs and pork loin; we feasted for a day or two, and shared with the neighbors. K's Papa really enjoyed eating stewed backbone. K made **Souse** by boiling the head with herbs and spices. Gelatin, which cooked out of the joints and cartilage, made the chilled souse hard enough to slice.

Bacon and sausage we ate fried for breakfast. Often we had sausage one day and sausage gravy the next day.

Fried Ham was more likely served at dinner. K cut a slice of ham for each person, put just a little grease in the cast iron skillet, and fried the ham quickly, turning it once or twice, till it was done all the way through.

Ham Gravy - Put the meat on a plate. Pour a cup of water into the skillet. Use a fork to scrape up any ham scraps and drippings. Pour into a bowl; each person can spoon this thin gravy onto their ham or onto a biscuit.

The pork we raised, along with a barnyard full of chickens, provided most of our meat. Milk and eggs were another source of high quality protein, as were peanuts, beans, cornbread, and such. Store-bought Beefsteak was a rare treat. An occasional **Squirrel or Rabbit** was fried like fried chicken or stewed like stewed chicken.

Fried Fish

Salt and pepper the fish and coat them in cornmeal.
Fry in hot grease in cast iron skillet till golden brown.

K cooked every fish we caught, no matter how small it was, but seldom was there enough for a meal. One time the creek dried up; fish were flopping in little puddles of water. Daddy tied a tow sack to a couple of little limbs and scooped the fish out. For once we had a big fish fry!

Fried Chicken

Cut chicken in pieces; roll in flour mixed with salt and pepper. Heat about an inch of grease in the cast iron skillet; add chicken after grease is hot. Cook over medium heat till brown outside and tender inside, but done all the way to the bone. Serve with Flour Gravy.

Flour Gravy

For $\frac{1}{4}$ cup hot grease from any fried meat, stir in 3 or 4 Tbsp. flour, enough to take up the grease. Keep stirring till the flour browns. Add salt and pepper. Pour in 2 cups milk and keep stirring till thick. If it gets too thick, add a little water. Serve on hot biscuits or mashed potatoes.

Chicken and Dumplings

Boil chicken till done; when you wiggle the drumstick it should "give" or even come apart at the joint. Remove the bones and skin. Bring the broth to a boil in a large boiler. Put in the chicken meat, a little salt and black pepper and some chopped onion. Make biscuit dough, recipe page 78; cut into little pieces, and drop into the boiling broth. Cover and cook 15 minutes till the dumplings are done.

Thanksgiving Dinner

Aunt Lucile always had Celery for Thanksgiving, and probably Turkey and Cranberry Sauce. K more likely cooked what we grew on the farm: Baked Sweet Potatoes, Green Beans, Homemade Lightbread with Peach Preserves, and Chicken and Dressing with Giblet Gravy.

Stewed Chicken

Use half as much water as for boiled chicken and let most of the water cook out. Use 2 Tbsp. flour for each cup liquid to make gravy if serving stewed meat with gravy.

Boiled Chicken

Cover chicken with water; boil with a little onion, salt, and pepper. Use broth to make dressing and giblet gravy.

Giblet Gravy

Boil the chicken giblets, which are the liver, heart, and gizzard, with a little salt and pepper; cook the neck with them. Chop the giblets, neck meat, and half a dozen boiled eggs and set aside.

Bring 4 cups chicken broth to a slow boil in a medium-sized boiler; it should have some fat in it. Mix 6 Tbsp. of flour into half a cup of cool water; stir all the lumps out. Slowly stir the flour mixture into the simmering broth. Cook till gravy thickens, about 15 minutes, stirring often. Stir in the chopped giblets and chopped boiled eggs. Add salt and black pepper to taste.

Chicken and Dressing

Remove stewed or boiled chicken from bones, mix into unbaked dressing, and bake at 450 degrees, 15 or 20 minutes until brown. Use K's dressing recipe on page 52.

K's Dressing

Margaret wrote home asking for K's Dressing recipe. This is a copy of K's answer written on K's typewriter.

Dressing.

You know how I dont measure

Crumble and mix two parts cornbread to one part biscuits or lightbread, till you have the amount you need.

Does your husband like onion? If so grate an onion in. I have to leave that out when Don is coming.

Sage and pepper and a little salt and chopped green pepper and celery

2 or 3 eggs, depending on how much you are making. Water enough to make it rather gooshy. You have to go by tast

Put it in the chicken or whatever.

Vegetables

Canning Corn

Lois says, "We had corn and more corn! We worked on the table outside (saw horses and long boards - the watermelon table) because it was so much cooler in the shade than inside the house. Any child that was big enough helped pull off the shucks; whatever age you were, there was a job that fit it. K cut off the corn in a wash tub. Cut down; prrrrt-scrape with the side of the knife; cut; prrrrt; cut; -- it is long, hard work to can what she canned. I see her lifting the heavy canner off the stove to let the pressure go down - she was melting with sweat and had a smile on her face. I have had some of the same sweat and smile when I was gardening and canning."

Fresh Garden Vegetables

Daddy plowed the garden; everybody helped plant and work it. We pulled fresh carrots, radishes, and green onions; sliced fresh tomatoes, cucumbers, and cantaloupe. The watermelon table held a place of honor in the back yard for cool-off afternoon snacks.

English peas did not grow well in our hot weather. When K managed to get a cooking of them it was a rare and special treat. Sometimes Aunt Lucile ate raw English peas! Can you imagine!

K picked fresh-shelled pinto beans when the pod was full but not dry. Shell the beans or purple hull peas, snap the green beans, wash the greens. Whichever it is, boil them in water; season with salt, pepper, and bacon grease. Mashed potatoes or corn on the cob need salt, pepper, and butter. K cut corn off the cob for Daddy and for canning.

Whether it was boiled cabbage, butterbeans, or turnip greens, K always drank the pot liquor. It has lots of vitamins and she didn't want to waste food.

I asked K, "Is it pot licker, like you lick the pot?"

"No, it's liquor with a q."

"Like in the liquor stores?!!"

"No, like liquid."

Dried Pinto Beans

Sort through dry beans and remove any broken or discolored ones. Soak overnight in about four times as much water as beans. Next morning bring to a boil; add salt and a ham bone with some ham scraps still on it. Cut the fire down and simmer till soft. We didn't have dried beans often; K's fresh shelled pintos were better.

Home-Canned Vegetables

K canned enough vegetables to last the winter; heated them up seasoned with salt and a little bacon grease.

Potato Soup

6 or 8 red potatoes
1 yellow onion
1 bunch multiplying onions
2 quarts water
2 tsp. salt
black pepper
¼ cup butter
½ cup milk

Chop potatoes and onions. Boil with salt, pepper, and butter until potatoes are very tender; leave some lumps of potato. After you put the milk in, heat but do not boil.

Potato Dumplings

9 medium potatoes
1 tsp. salt
3 eggs
2/3 cup bread crumbs
1 cup flour
½ tsp. nutmeg

Boil potatoes in jackets till soft. Remove skins and mash the potatoes. Mix everything together and make into balls; drop in boiling water. When the dumplings come to the surface, boil 3 minutes, uncovered. Serve dumplings with the broth they cooked in.

Fried Potatoes

Slice potatoes into cast iron skillet; add chopped onion. Cook in a little hot grease stirring occasionally. When potatoes begin to brown, turn heat down, put a lid on the pan, and cook slowly till soft and lightly browned, stirring now and then. Salt and pepper.

Baked Sweet Potatoes

K scrubbed the sweet potatoes clean, put them in the biscuit pan, and baked them at 350 degrees for over an hour. They came out of the oven very soft. Some of the natural sugar caramelized and made a sticky brown spot on the bottom of each potato. That was the best part.

Winnsboro was sweet potato country, and Daddy grew some good ones. Somebody tried to tell him to sell the good ones and let his family eat the culls. Daddy said, "My family is just as important as anybody else. I'm keeping some nice, pretty potatoes for us, too." It may not have been good business sense, but we sure did enjoy them.

Grandma Lila's Squash

2 cups chicken broth
½ a medium onion, chopped
4 medium-sized potatoes, sliced thin
4 medium-sized squash, sliced

Bring chicken broth to a simmering boil. Add the onion and let it cook while you wash, peel and slice the potatoes. Let them cook till potatoes are more than half done. Add the sliced squash and cook until the squash is barely done. Add a little salt and a good bit of black pepper. K said, "Mama never cooked squash any way but this."

Wilted Lettuce - Tear loose-leaf garden lettuce in bite-sized pieces; drizzle with hot bacon grease and stir in a little vinegar. Sprinkle crisp crumbled bacon on top. When home-grown lettuce got bitter, it was still good this way.

Cucumber Pickles

K picked cucumbers of all different sizes and made all different kinds of pickles. She sliced some big ones for bread and butter pickles with a spicy, sweet-and-sour flavor. Small cucumbers with homegrown heads of dill seed made whole dill pickles. Brine-cured pickles were packed down with salt in the old crock churn for a couple of weeks, like sauerkraut. Sometimes when we had lots of cucumbers we picked the tiny baby ones about the size of your little finger and K made crisp sweet gherkins! She soaked the little cucumbers in alum water to make them crisp. Those little baby pickles were my favorite.

Chow-Chow

Just before the first frost, you'll need to pick the last of everything that's left in the garden. If you have some green tomatoes, a few odds and ends of cucumbers, some onions, and a small cabbage or two, you could make chow-chow. Wash everything and run it through the sausage grinder; mix in a few spoons of salt, and let it set a few hours to draw some of the water out of the vegetables. Drain the water off and put the vegetables in a big cooking pot. Add vinegar and sugar, half as much sugar as vinegar, until it just barely covers the vegetables. Put in a tablespoon of pickling spices and a teaspoon of ground turmeric. Cook till vegetables are tender. Put into jars, boiling hot, and seal with canning jar lids. Now-a-days they tell you to process for ten minutes in a boiling water bath.

Old-fashioned Chow-chow is good with peas or beans or anything that needs a touch of relish.

Sauerkraut

K wrote, "Papa made very good gardens. Especially cabbages. They would have won at the Fair, if the Fair had been at that time of the year. We made so much good sauerkraut in those days. Mama would cut the cabbage very thin, and our job was to punch it down in the big churn to salt and ferment it."

The recipe I have says to mix 4 tablespoons salt with 10 quarts of shredded cabbage. The salt drew water from the cabbage and formed a natural brine. When the salted cabbage came to about 3 or 4 inches from the top of the churn, they covered it with a clean, white cuptowel and put a plate that fit snuggly inside the churn, with a gallon jar full of water on top to weigh it down and keep the cabbage covered with brine.

They let the cabbage ferment in a warm room for about two weeks. Little gas bubbles coming up to the top showed that fermentation was taking place. Every day they had to change the cloth and wash it, skim off anything that floated to the top, and adjust the weight. When bubbles stopped coming to the surface, it was ready to eat, and they canned the sauerkraut in quart jars. My recipe says to process in boiling water bath for 20 minutes.

Sauerkraut and Wieners

This was one of our favorite meals. Cut a package of store-bought hot dogs into bite-sized pieces and brown in the skillet just a little bit. Add a quart jar of sauerkraut. Cook it down till most of the juice is gone and the kraut is tender. Eat it while it's hot.

Fruit

Fresh Fruit

On the Winnsboro farm we grew grapes, peaches, pears, plums, blackberries, strawberries, and cantaloupes. Friends shared apples and figs. "And the Lord God took the man and put him in the garden of Eden to tend and keep it. And the Lord God commanded the man, saying, 'Of every tree of the garden you may freely eat....'"

We did eat freely. And we tended the garden.

1. What is the oldest job in the world? Gardening.

2. Who was the first gardener in the world?

Did you say Adam? Look in Genesis 2:8 and see who planted the first garden. Adam did cause a lot of trouble when he ate from that *one* tree God said not to eat from.

Canned Fruit

K set herself a goal to can a hundred quarts of each kind of fruit and vegetable, enough to last all year. How many blackberries would you have to pick to fill a hundred quarts? Daddy built a big basement room at the Winnsboro house with rows and rows of freestanding shelves, like at the library, to store the jars of food.

Much of the canned fruit went into pies, preserves, and jelly, but often K just poured a jar of pears or peaches into a bowl and served them along with the meal. She never made salads with them; we just spooned some onto our plate. They were good!

Fruit Salad

When the Paris relatives came to visit, they brought apples, oranges, and bananas; fruit we didn't grow. Those same three fruits were always in our Christmas stockings. We remember fruit salad usually at Christmas dinner, maybe Thanksgiving or some other special occasion. Fruit salad was chopped-up apples, oranges, and bananas.

Pears and Sweet Potatoes

K put layers of home-canned pears and cooked sweet potatoes in the biscuit pan. She sprinkled on a generous amount of brown sugar, a little cinnamon, and dabs of butter, and put it in the oven till it was bubbly.

You can substitute pears and apples for each other in many recipes; pear butter is almost the same as apple butter. Apples do not hold together well enough to substitute for pear preserves.

Baked Apples

K cut the stems out of the apples with a paring knife then dug out the cores with a spoon so it wouldn't make a hole all the way through the bottom. She set the apples in the biscuit pan and put a big spoonful of sugar inside each one with a sprinkle of cinnamon and laid a pat of butter on top. Pour about an inch of water in the bottom of the pan. Bake 350 degrees for 45 minutes or more, until very tender. Depending on the variety of the apple, some cook quicker than others.

Apple Butter

Peel, quarter, and core apples. Use enough water to half-way cover the apples. Cook at a slow boil till apples get soft; stir often so they don't scorch. When most of the water is gone, mash with the potato masher. At this point the apples will look like lumpy applesauce. Add sugar and spices; how much you need will depend on how sweet or tart your apples were, and on your personal taste. Start with $\frac{1}{2}$ cup sugar for each 4 cups of applesauce, with 1 tsp. cinnamon, $\frac{1}{2}$ tsp. nutmeg, and $\frac{1}{4}$ tsp. cloves. Taste and add more if needed. Lower heat and keep on stirring till thick.

Fruit Butter Tests for Doneness:

1. Put a spoonful on a plate and let it sit a minute; if you see liquid seeping out around the edges, keep cooking.
2. As you are stirring, bring swirls and spoonfuls up on top. If they hold their shape for a minute, it's probably done.
3. Final test - Taste some. Is it the way *you* like it?

Seal in mason jars by manufacturer's directions.

Pear Butter can be made by the Apple Butter recipe; just use pears instead of apples.

Apple Jelly

Wash apples, cut out stems and bad spots, cut into pieces but do not peel or core. Your jelly will jell better if you use some under-ripe apples in with the sweet ones; the immature apples have more pectin than the ripe ones. Add peels and cores from making apple butter. Add enough water to half-way cover the apples and boil, stirring often, till they are soft. K spread a clean cuptowel inside her jelly-stand colander, poured the contents of the pan into it, and let the juice drip through. Then she gathered up the cuptowel to wring out all the juice she could. Some recipes will tell you not to squeeze juice out because it makes the jelly cloudy, but we didn't care how it looked and K didn't want to waste any of that good juice. For each cup of juice, add a cup of sugar. Bring to a boil and stir till sugar dissolves. Boil over high heat, stirring often, till it passes the apple jelly test.

Apple jelly test: Dip a cool metal spoon into the boiling jelly. Raise the spoon above the steam and let the liquid drip back into the pan. If the jelly hangs off the edge of the spoon then comes off all in one sheet, it's done. The old folks said, "Cook till liquid sheets from a metal spoon."

Pour hot jelly up in jars with two-piece canning lids and seal according to manufacturer's directions.

Old Fashioned Cooked-Down Fruit Jelly

Grape, Blackberry, Plum, Peach, Pear, Strawberry

You can make any fruit jelly by the Apple Jelly recipe.

The fruit pulp left in the cuptowel after the juice is squeezed out can be worked through the colander and added to fruit butter. Or you could eat it like applesauce. Feed the peel and core residue to the chickens.

Pear Preserves

10 cups pears, peeled, cored, and cut in small slices
10 cups sugar
1 lemon, sliced thin
Mix and let sit till sugar draws some juice from the fruit. Bring to a bubbling boil in a large heavy pan. Stir often; when preserves begin to thicken up, stir constantly. Pear preserves will slowly turn a beautiful amber color. When the preserves look thick, test to see if they are done.
Test for doneness:
Dip a metal spoon and let the liquid drip back into the pan.
1. If it runs off like water, keep cooking and stirring.
2. If it takes a while for a drop to gather and slowly drip, it is probably done. "Liquid sheets from a metal spoon."
3. If it starts trying to spin a thread, you've cooked it too long. The preserves will be good, but when they cool they'll be thick like taffy candy. Seal in mason jars with two-piece lids according to manufacturer's directions.

Fig Preserves

10 cups figs, stems removed
10 cups sugar
1 lemon, sliced thin
Cook same as recipe for Pear Preserves above.

Peach Preserves

Peel peaches and cut in slices. Use half as much sugar as you have peaches. Cook at a low boil, stirring constantly till thick. Seal in mason jars with two piece canning lids.

Strawberry Preserves

Wash berries, remove stem end. Cook like Peach Preserves

Watermelon Rind Preserves

After eating the watermelon, cut rind into ½ in. strips. Trim away all the hard green part and most of the red; leave just a little pink for color. Cut into ½ inch cubes.

10 cups chopped rind
10 cups sugar
1 lemon, sliced thin

Mix and allow to sit till it juices up, then boil, stirring often.When preserves begin to thicken up, stir constantly. Cook until liquid sheets from a metal spoon. Seal in jars.

Pickled Peach Seeds

Lois wanted some pickled peaches. Somebody out in the country said, "I have Indian Peaches coming ripe. How many do you want?" Lois said two bushels. Indian Peaches are really good for pickling, but they are small, and the more they picked, the smaller they got. So there we were peeling all those little bitty peaches. Actually, they turned out pretty good, once they got pickled and canned. We ate them all winter and really enjoyed them, but Mat carried Lois high, laughing at her Pickled Peach Seeds.

Pickled Peaches

8 cups sugar
4 cups vinegar
2 cups water
8 cinnamon sticks
2 Tbsp. whole cloves
8 pounds peaches, peeled

Put everything but peaches in large pan; simmer 5 minutes. Add peaches and boil until they are fork tender. Put the peaches in jars; pour hot syrup to cover fruit. Make sure to get some cloves and cinnamon sticks in each jar. Seal. For best flavor, allow to sit a week or two before using.

Green Tomato Mincemeat

3 pounds green tomatoes	6 cups sugar
3 pounds apples	2 Tbsp. salt
2 pounds raisins	2 tsp. cloves
1 cup vinegar	1 tsp. nutmeg
1 cup water	2 tsp. cinnamon

Grind tomatoes in food chopper, discard juice. Grind apples and raisins. (You can use pears and/or apples.) Mix everything in a large jelly pan. Cook, stirring constantly, until thick. Use Apple Butter test for doneness, page 61. Seal in jars by manufacturer's directions.

Make two-crust pie using 1 pint of mincemeat.

Candied Orange Peel

Peel 3 oranges for about 1 cup of peels. Snip small. Cover with about 3 cups water. Bring to a good boil then stir in 1 tsp. baking soda; it will foam up. Stir a minute then pour off water. This step removes some of the harsh acid taste of the peels. Add fresh water, boil, stir, pour off. This step rinses off the baking soda. Add 1 cup sugar. Cook and stir till water cooks out and it looks jelled. Pour onto a buttered plate to cool. Candied Lemon Peel can be made the same way. Candied Peel can be stored at room temperature for a few days. Good to nibble on like candy, put in a batch of cookies, or bake in fruitcake.

K said that when she was a girl, she thought all the oranges grew at the North Pole, because the only time they got oranges was in their Christmas stockings. Candied orange peel was one way to keep enjoying that good taste and aroma after the oranges were gone.

Persimmons

Farmers cussed the sassafras and persimmon trees; they spent hours with the grubbing hoe digging sprouts from their fields. Thank goodness, some of them escaped.

We watched the little persimmon trees in the fence rows and along the country roadways as autumn leaves fell and the fruit became more visible, but we didn't dare take a taste till after a really good frost. Have you ever tasted a green persimmon? Something in the frost and the cold changes them from a hard, bitter, astringent, mouth-puckering disaster to a soft, sweet, dark brown, wrinkled, mellow, really-good-tasting fruit. When we found some good ones, we ate some, and then we took some home to K. Just a few, once a year.

Sassafras Tea

A sassafras leaf may have two lobes like a mitten, three lobes, or one lobe. You'll usually find all three leaf shapes on the same tree. Daddy kept the grubbing hoe in the trunk of the car during sassafras season. When he found some, he stopped and dug up a few roots. It's okay to get them anytime after the sap goes down in the fall and before the sap rises in the spring. That way the sap is in the roots, giving them more strength and flavor.

K washed the roots real good, put them in a boiler, covered the roots with water, and set them to simmer on the back of the stove. Whenever she poured up a cup of the tea, she put more water in the pan and let it keep on simmering. Sassafras tea has long been considered a spring tonic, but we drank it all winter long. It has a mild root beer flavor. Sweeten to taste with sugar or honey.

Milk & Eggs

G's Milk Cow

G wrote: "When we moved into town at Commerce, Daddy rented some space in a pasture and barn at the edge of town for the cow. That may have been the same cow he bought at Greenville with my hay bailing money. He said if I would loan him $87 to buy the cow, he would pay me back when he could or when he sold the cow. I haven't seen that cow for many years, but it would appear that he has not yet sold it.

"I walked over a mile each way, twice a day, to do the milking. I was quite good at it, and actually enjoyed it except on very cold mornings, or extremely hot afternoons, or when there were cuckle burrs in the swishing tail. Even then, it was alright, because we surely enjoyed the good milk, butter, buttermilk, and charsh."

Charsh

K skimmed the cream from a gallon jar of milk and set it on the kitchen table until it clabbered; that is, the curds separated from the whey. K put a cuptowel over a wide-mouth gallon jar and pushed it into the jar a little bit to make a pouch. Lila held the cuptowel in place while K poured the clabber in. Most of the whey drained through right away, then K put the lid on the jar and let it drip some more. After a while she took the cuptowel out to the clothesline. She carefully rolled the top of the cloth pouch to keep the milk curds in, laid the folded flap over the clothesline, and fastened it securely with four or five clothespins. It hung there dripping and drying for several hours. An old pan sat under the clothesline to catch the dripping whey. The chickens perched on the edges of the pan drinking all the whey that dripped into it.

When K brought the bag back in the kitchen, the milk solids were rather firm and she scraped them into a bowl. K stirred in salt, pepper, and some chopped onion, "and that's charsh!" she said. It was a German word; the word and the recipe came to us from K's Papa's German family, and K was the only person we knew who made it.

Lila told us, "When they sell this at the store, they call it cottage cheese, only it isn't as good as K's."

"Well, they don't put the onion in, for one thing," K said modestly.

"And this is fresh and homemade." I added. "Homemade is always better than store-bought."

Churning Buttermilk

K had a big crock churn with a wooden dasher for churning butter. The dasher was a round wooden stick (probably cut from a perfectly good broomstick after the broom wore out) about three feet long with a wooden piece shaped like a big plus sign nailed on the bottom of it. K poured clabbered milk into the churn, set the freshly-washed dasher in it, and put the dasher-handle through the hole in the center of the churn lid. The dasher had to be pumped up and down for about 30 or 40 minutes till the butter separated from the milk. K spooned the butter out, rinsed and salted it, and put it in the butter dish on the kitchen table. Then she poured the buttermilk into gallon jars.

K used buttermilk in her cooking, especially when baking cornbread and biscuits. Daddy crumbled cornbread into his buttermilk and ate it with a spoon. I liked it that way, too; and I always chose buttermilk to drink rather than sweet milk. People called it sweet milk, not that it tasted sweet like sugar, but because it wasn't sour like buttermilk.

If you don't have a churn, you can make butter by shaking a half pint of whipping cream in a quart jar till the butter separates from the whey. Pour off the whey and rinse the butter with cool water. Mash with a spoon to get all the water out. Stir in some salt. Serve on bread or crackers for a tasty treat. I've done this with church and school groups, as well as at home with children and grandchildren, and we always enjoyed it.

Hot Chocolate

1/3 cup cocoa
1/3 cup sugar
4 cups milk
$\frac{1}{2}$ tsp. vanilla

Lois showed me how to make hot chocolate. The problem is, if you just pour the milk in all at once, the cocoa will lump up and it'll be hard to get the lumps out. So you mix the dry cocoa and sugar together real good then slowly stir in the milk. Lois poured half a cup of milk at the edge of the cocoa and sugar mixture, then she stirred round and round right at the edge of the cocoa till it all got mixed in. Then she poured in the rest of the milk and kept stirring while it heated up. Hot enough to warm us up, but not hot enough to burn a tongue.

Milk Toast

K made milk toast only when we were sick. Margaret said, "It was almost worth being sick for." K spread a generous amount of butter on a slice of bread and toasted it in the oven while heating a cup of milk in the little pan. As soon as the toast got brown she put it in a bowl, poured the warm milk over it and served it warm. The aroma of bread toasting, the warm buttery milk, the soft bread with an occasional crispy spot, and the warm comfort of K bringing something special to make us feel better - all of these are precious memories.

Milk toast, ice cream, and Jello soothe a sore throat and are especially helpful after you've had your tonsils out.

Ice Cream for 1 gallon freezer

4 eggs
2 cups sugar
2 cups light cream
2 teaspoons vanilla, or to taste
Dash of salt
Add milk to within $1\frac{1}{2}$ inches of top. Add fruit before milk.

K beat the eggs adding a little sugar at a time, till all the sugar got mixed in and the eggs were light and fluffy. Back in the '40s, everybody said "the sugar cooks the eggs." Light cream is like half and half. Cream rose to the top when a bucket of milk, fresh from the cow, sat undisturbed overnight. The cook scooped heavy cream off the top, then light cream which was half cream, half milk.

Stir everything together and pour it into the ice-cream freezer can. Pour in milk, but leave $1\frac{1}{2}$ inches space at the top. K added ripe peaches, strawberries, or blackberries when they were in season. Add fruit before milk.

Daddy walked down to the country store with a tow sack, bought a block of ice, and toted it home on his shoulder. It was always a hot day and much of the ice melted on the way home dripping down his back. Daddy just laughed and said, "Well, I won't need a bath today." He chipped ice from the block with the ice-pick and packed ice and rock salt into the hand-cranked freezer.

A little child sat on a folded towel on top of the freezer while a big one turned the crank; when nobody could turn it anymore, the ice cream was ready to eat.

Fried Eggs were a staple for breakfast. K fixed them hard, soft, or runny; whichever way we wanted them. Daddy took his eggs hard, so Lois wanted hers hard, too. Daddy left many good examples for his children to follow.

Egg Gravy - Make flour gravy with bacon grease. Toward the end of the cooking time, crack a couple of eggs and stir them in real fast. When the eggs look done, take two fresh hot biscuits. Put egg gravy on one; butter the other one to eat with preserves, honey, or molasses.

Beviled Eggs - Most people would spell that with a D, but we aren't gonna say that word. We didn't usually have salad dressing, sometimes we had mustard, but whatever K had (pickle juice or relish, salt, pepper), she mixed it into the yolks, spooned them back into the whites, and we had a picnic, even if we ate it at the kitchen table.

When the neighbor's cow went dry, we shared them a bucket of milk every day till their cow "came in fresh" again. They did the same for us. At Winnsboro we had several cows; when one went dry, the others kept producing. Daddy sold milk to the cheese factory.

When the Watkins man came by the house, K usually bought vanilla and maybe cinnamon or nutmeg, but one time she did something special: she bought orange, lemon, and strawberry flavorings. Each child got to choose which one we wanted, and K put a few drops in our glass of milk. We added a little sugar. Stir it in and enjoy! Just a little something different made a special treat.

Bread

K's Lightbread

One of K's earliest memories was about making pretend lightbread. She wrote, "Mama and Papa were sitting on the front steps and I was at the end of the steps making lightbread with dirt, as close to Mama as I could get. The moon had been shining real bright but a cloud suddenly came over it and I asked, 'Where moon?' I can't see Papa in this memory but I can still hear him laugh. He said, 'Your lightbread rose so high it got between us and the moon!' "

K was probably 3 years old. She said, "I can remember it as plain as if it was yesterday."

When K made yeast-rising bread for our family, she used the recipe on the back of the yeast package.

Lightbread Recipe on back of yeast package

6 cups all-purpose flour
2 envelopes dry yeast
$1\frac{1}{2}$ cups water
3 Tbsp. sugar
$\frac{1}{2}$ cup milk
2 Tbsp. butter
2 tsp. salt

Place $\frac{1}{4}$ cup warm water (100° to 110°F) in a large warm bowl. Sprinkle in yeast and 1 teaspoon sugar; stir. Let sit 5 to 10 minutes, until foamy on top. Add remaining water, milk, butter, sugar, salt and 4 cups flour. Mix well, scraping bowl occasionally. Add more flour, a little at a time, till you have a soft dough. (You don't have to use all the flour. The dough should be tender but not sticky.) Knead on lightly floured surface until smooth and elastic, about 8 to 10 minutes. Place in a greased bowl, turning once to grease top. Cover; let rise in a warm, draft-free place until doubled in size, about 45 minutes to an hour.

Punch down; divide dough in half. Roll out each half to 12 x 7-inch rectangle. Roll up each rectangle as for jelly roll. Pinch seams to seal. Place, seam sides down, in greased $8\frac{1}{2}$ x $4\frac{1}{2}$ inch loaf pans. Cover; let rise in warm, draft-free place until doubled in size, about 45 minutes. Bake at 400°F for 25 to 30 minutes till done.

K didn't always buy fresh yeast each time she made bread. She often saved a lump of bread dough to start the next batch with. Like Jesus said, a little lump of yeast will make the whole loaf rise.

Yeast-Rising Doughnuts 1950

When we walked in the back door after school, the whole kitchen smelled like sweet yeast bread rising.

"Doughnuts!" Margaret and I said together.

K was punching down the dough from its first rise then she started rolling it out on the bread board.

"Have you seen the doughnut-hole cutter?" K asked.

"I saw it in the drawer with the can opener and the egg turner last night when I was drying the dishes," Margaret said. She found it and K twisted it into the middle of the biscuit cutter and started cutting out doughnuts. Margaret and I made rows of the "holes" while K laid out the doughnuts until we had the table almost covered with them. We changed out of our school clothes and ran outside to play while we waited for the doughnuts to rise.

K dropped a doughnut into the hot grease, and in a minute when it floated up to the top, she turned it over with a fork. She had two skillets going, and as soon as she took out one golden brown doughnut and put it on the folded cuptowel to drain, she dropped in another one. We all took turns shaking the hot doughnuts in a brown paper sack with sugar in it. Another sack had sugar with a little cinnamon; that's the one I liked best. We ate most of the doughnuts warm, as soon as we got the sugar on them.

That was supper for that day.

K used the lightbread recipe on page 74 for her doughnuts, except she increased the sugar to $\frac{1}{2}$ cup. Allow the cut-out doughnuts to rise 30 to 45 minutes.

A Doughnut Song

We sang this to the tune of "Turkey in the Straw"

Well, I went to Cooper and I walked around the block;
And I walked right in to the Doughnut Shop;
I picked two Doughnuts out of the Grease,
And I handed the Clerk a Five-Cent Piece.
She looked at the Nickel, and she looked at me,
Said she, "This Nickel is no good for me;
It has a Hole in the middle,
and it's all the way through!"
Said I, "The Doughnut has a Hole in it, too!"
Shave and a haircut, two bits!

Hot Rolls

K sometimes used one cup of whole wheat flour to give her hot rolls color and texture. In the early years she used a cup of graham flour as part of the measure for flour, using the Lightbread recipe from page 74. Pinch off enough dough to halfway fill each cup in lightly greased muffin tins. Let rise about 30 minutes, till doubled. Bake at 400 degrees for 15 minutes or until golden brown.

Cinnamon Rolls

Use the Lightbread recipe on page 74. Increase sugar to ½ cup. After you roll out two 12 x 7-inch rectangles, spread a mixture of ½ cup butter, 1 cup sugar, and 2 tsp. cinnamon on the bread dough. Butter needs to be soft. Roll up. Cut into one inch slices. Put cut side down in greased pans. Let rise 30 minutes. Bake at 375 degrees for 20 to 25 minutes until lightly browned and bubbly.

Kuchen

1 pkg. yeast
1 cup milk
1 cup butter
$\frac{1}{2}$ cup sugar
2 large eggs
4 cups flour
1 tsp. salt

Dissolve yeast in 2 Tbsp. lukewarm water. Scald the milk, and pour it into a large mixing bowl. Add the butter and sugar, and stir until the butter is melted. Beat in the eggs. When the mixture has cooled to lukewarm, add the dissolved yeast. Mix in the salt and 4 cups of flour, 2 cups at a time. Turn the dough out on a lightly floured surface and knead, working in a little extra flour if the dough feels too sticky. Continue to knead until the dough is soft, smooth, and elastic, about 2 minutes. Put the dough in a greased bowl, turning it to coat the surface. Cover the bowl, place it in a warm spot, and leave it until the dough has doubled in bulk, about 1$\frac{1}{4}$ hours. Turn dough out onto lightly floured breadboard. Knead just a little while, then divide into two loaf pans. Allow to rise till doubled. Bake at 350 degrees until golden and the bread sounds hollow when rapped with your knuckle, about 45 minutes.

Kuchen, the German word for coffee cake, is a lightly sweet yeast bread, rich with butter and eggs. It can be sprinkled with spices and dried fruits and rolled up jelly-roll style, baked in a ring pan, formed into a braid, or shaped into rolls. K's was a slightly flattened loaf.

Fried Bread

K made biscuit dough, patted it out about half as thick as for biscuits, cut it into strips about 1" by 3" and fried them in bacon grease till lightly brown, turning them over once or twice. We ate them with syrup, honey, or jelly.

K Made the Biscuits

Five-year-old Katie loved being in the kitchen watching her Mama cook. She stood on a chair while Mama made the breakfast biscuits. Soon she learned the routine; she handed Mama the box of soda when it was time for it, then the baking powder. She begged, "Let me do it", and Mama watched her sift the flour and work the dough until Katie knew what it meant to "add enough flour until it feels right." She learned to measure the salt, soda, and baking powder in the palm of her hand. She scooped out enough shortening and worked it into the flour with her fingers. Before long Mama stood there watching while Katie did the whole thing "all by herself!" Her biscuits came out of the oven tender, brown, and beautiful. From then on it was Katie's job to make the breakfast biscuits, and she loved it. K still loved it after she grew up, cooking for her own children.

Buttermilk Biscuits

2 cups flour	1 tsp. salt
3 tsp. baking powder,	1/3 cup shortening
½ tsp. baking soda	2/3 cup buttermilk

Work shortening into sifted dry ingredients until like coarse crumbs. Stir in the buttermilk till it makes a soft dough. Sprinkle flour on the bread board and knead a bit. Pat the dough about half an inch thick and cut with biscuit cutter. Bake in greased biscuit pan at 450 degrees, for 10 to 15 minutes till biscuits are nicely browned.

That is the recipe, but here is how K always made biscuits:

K's Biscuits in the Flour Pan

K emptied the sack of flour into the big flour pan; that's where the flour was stored. She worked her biscuits right there on top of the flour in the pan. Each day K scooped up flour with the flour sifter and sifted out any hard pieces left from the day before, quickly working through the top few inches of flour; then she made a little well in the top of the flour. She measured the salt into the palm of her hand, put it in the well, then the baking powder; she mashed the soda in her hand with the back of a spoon, to get the lumps out then put it in and stirred it up just a little bit. She scooped enough shortening out of the shortening can with her fingers, worked it into the flour then added the buttermilk a little at a time, working it in each time. She worked the whole ball around a little while, until it was firm enough she could pick it up, but still very tender, and put it out on the lightly floured breadboard, patted it out with her hand, and cut the biscuits with her tin biscuit cutter. Her biscuit pan was 13 inches by 9 inches so she likely made twice as much as my recipe says. She melted a little shortening in the pan, turned each biscuit upside down as she put it in the pan, to grease the top of each one, then put the pan in the oven.

K made biscuits every morning for breakfast served with honey, molasses, jelly, preserves, and often sausage gravy. We saved leftover biscuits to make bread pudding.

When the Paris people came to visit us in the country, they always said, "What a treat! Homemade biscuits and fresh cornbread every day!" When we visited them in town we said, "Oh, boy! Store-bought sliced bread!"

Homemade Egg Noodles

3 cups flour
3 eggs
½ tsp. salt
3 Tbsp. warm water

Sift flour and salt onto dough board; make a well. Break the eggs into the well and gradually work them into the flour. Add water and work it in. Knead about a minute. Work in more flour if dough is sticky, but not too much; you want dough to be tender and elastic. Divide in thirds. Roll paper thin. Sprinkle with flour; let stand 15 minutes. Roll up; cut ¼ inch strips. Spread strips ½ inch apart on floured cuptowel. Dry two hours. Stir into gently boiling water; cook about 10 minutes until tender.

K made noodles on top of the flour pan, like she did the biscuits. She made a little well in the top of the flour added salt, dropped in an egg, mixed it in, then broke in another. She mixed in the water one spoonful at a time, then kept working the ball until it was firm enough she could pick it up, put it onto the breadboard, and knead it.

Hotcakes

1¼ cups flour
2 tsp. baking powder
½ tsp. soda
½ tsp. salt
1 egg
1 cup buttermilk

Sift together dry ingredients. Stir buttermilk and egg together; stir into flour mixture. Melt a little shortening in a cast iron skillet; pour in ¼ cup hotcake batter. Cook till dry around the edges and full of bubbles on top. Turn over with egg turner to brown other side. Serve with butter and a choice of honey, molasses, or jelly.

Cornbread

2 Tbsp. bacon grease
1 egg
1¼ cups buttermilk
1 cup cornmeal
½ cup flour
2 tsp. baking powder
½ tsp. salt
½ tsp. soda

Put the bacon grease into a 10 inch cast-iron skillet. Put the skillet in the oven to preheat while the oven is preheating to 450 degrees.

Stir the milk and egg together; break the egg yolk so it will mix in good. Sift the dry ingredients together into a bowl. When the oven is heated, stir the milk and egg into the dry ingredients. Pour immediately into the hot skillet; it should be hot enough to sizzle. Bake at 450 degrees for 15 to 20 minutes till done, lightly browned.

We always had biscuits for breakfast, cornbread for dinner, and leftover cornbread and biscuits for supper. Leftover cornbread made a good afternoon snack with a fresh-from-the-garden radish or onion.

Cornmeal Mush

2 cups water
¼ cup cornmeal

Stir the cornmeal and a little salt into cool water. If you pour the cornmeal into hot water, it will lump up. Bring to a boil, cook and stir like cream of wheat till thick. Serve warm with butter and honey. Or eat it with salt and pepper, a spoonful of butter, and a little milk.

K said, "This is like the porridge Goldilocks and the Three Bears had. Eat it up; it's goo-ood!"

Cornbread Hotcakes

1 cup cornmeal
½ cup flour
2 tsp. baking powder
½ tsp. soda
1 tsp. salt
1½ cups buttermilk
1 egg
bacon grease

Sift together dry ingredients. Stir in buttermilk and egg. Put a little bacon grease in a cast iron skillet over medium heat. Cook like you would hotcakes. Eat with a meal, as you would regular baked cornbread, or eat as hotcakes with sorghum molasses. We didn't have these often.

Grandma Julia's Hoe Cake

Grandma Julia rejoiced when she saw there was a fireplace in her room. "I'll cook me a hoe cake!" she said as she got a nice fire going. It was January, and we had just moved into the house at the Winnsboro farm. Grandma went outside and got the shovel and washed it clean. By then the fire had burned down to a nice bed of hot coals. She made up a small recipe of cornbread dough, put it on the clean shovel, and set it on the bed of coals to cook. "I used to cook like this all time when ye daddy was a little boy!" Grandma said. "Back then I had me a bake oven in the fireplace, and my big ol' dinner pot. Bread cooked in that oven tasted better than any I cooked in the stove."

Grandma Julia was Daddy's Mama. She lived with our family from soon after K and Daddy married in 1928 till she passed away in February of 1940. Lila said, "Grandma Julia was a funny little hill country woman, but she loved me and I loved her. She paid me more attention than anybody else did. I asked her how it was in the old days and she told me the most that she knew."

Cakes

Uncle Victor's Cake

Lila and Lois went to spend a week at Aunt Lucile's house. They had been there for several hours when Uncle Victor started snooping around the kitchen like he was looking for something. "You mean these girls have been here all this time and we don't have a cake yet?" he teased. They took the hint. Uncle Victor soon had his cake, made from scratch of course. Uncle Victor was as liberal with his praise as he was with his cake servings. He was a special person in our lives, and we loved him dearly.

Yellow Cake

1 cup butter	3 cups flour
2 cups sugar	½ tsp. soda
3 eggs	1 Tbsp. baking powder
1 cup buttermilk	1 tsp. vanilla

Cream butter and sugar; add eggs, beating well after each one. Alternate sifted dry ingredients and milk. Stir in vanilla. Bake 350 degrees for 25 to 30 minutes, till done.

Tests to see if cake is done:

1. Cake begins to draw away from edges of the pan.
2. A broom straw inserted in center comes out clean.
3. Cake springs back when touched lightly in center.

Chocolate Fudge Icing

3 cups sugar	1 can evaporated milk
¾ cup cocoa	¾ cup butter
	1 tsp. vanilla

Mix sugar, cocoa, and milk in pan. Bring to a boil and cook to soft ball stage. Remove from heat. Add butter and vanilla. Beat until thick enough to spread.

Chocolate Fudge Cake

Bake a regular yellow sheet cake. Near end of baking time, cook chocolate fudge icing, above. As soon as the cake comes out of the oven, poke a hole in the hot cake with a fork, pour in Chocolate Fudge Icing while icing is still hot, not thick. Poke another hole in the cake, pour in icing, till cake is dotted with holes full of icing. Then pour the rest of the fudge on top of the cake. This was my favorite cake that K made. Well, next to the fruitcake.

Chocolate Layer Cake

2½ cups flour
1 cup cocoa
1½ tsp. soda
½ tsp. baking powder
½ tsp. salt
1 cup butter
1¾ cups sugar
3 eggs
1¼ tsp. vanilla
1 2/3 cups milk

Cream butter and sugar; add eggs, beating well after each one; stir in vanilla. Add sifted dry ingredients alternately with milk. Pour into two greased and floured cake pans. Bake at 350 degrees for 30 to 35 minutes till done.

Do not open the oven during the first 15 minutes the cake is baking; it could make the cake fall. We were told jumping near the stove could make the cake fall, too.

Boiled Icing

Mix one cup of granulated sugar with one-fourth of a cup of milk. Stir until it boils; then let it boil for five minutes without stirring. Remove from heat; add one teaspoon vanilla. While it is cooling, stir or beat it constantly and it will become a thick, creamy frosting.

Powdered Sugar Icing

1 box powdered sugar
¼ cup butter
1 tsp. vanilla
6 Tbsp. canned milk

Mix sugar, butter, and vanilla. Add milk a little at a time until icing is easy to spread. Spread over cake.

Chocolate Powdered Sugar Icing

Add 4 Tablespoons cocoa to make Chocolate icing.

Spice Cake

1 cup sugar
¾ cup molasses
2/3 cup shortening
1 1/3 cups buttermilk
2 ½ cups flour
2 tsp. baking powder
1½ tsp. baking soda
1 tsp. salt
1 tsp. ginger
1 tsp. cinnamon
½ tsp. allspice
½ tsp. cloves
½ tsp. nutmeg
3 large eggs

Cream together sugar, molasses, and shortening. Sift dry ingredients. Add alternately with buttermilk. Beat eggs into batter one at a time, beating well after each addition. Pour into lightly greased and floured 13" by 9" pan. Bake at 350 degrees for 45 minutes, or until cake tests done.

Gingerbread

½ cup butter
1 cup sugar
1 cup molasses
1 cup buttermilk
2 eggs
3 cups flour
1 tsp. baking soda
2 tsp. ginger
2 tsp. cinnamon
½ tsp. nutmeg

Cream butter and sugar; beat in eggs; stir in milk and molasses. Sift dry ingredients together; add a little at a time, mixing well. Bake in greased pan at 350 degrees, 50 to 60 minutes till done.

Sugar was rationed from 1942 -1947 because of the war. Many recipes then replaced sugar with molasses or honey. *Try making this gingerbread recipe with 1½ cups of molasses and no sugar.

Pound Cake

1 cup butter
1 cup sugar
4 large eggs
2 cups flour
½ tsp. salt
1½ tsp. baking powder
1 cup milk
1 tsp vanilla

Cream butter and sugar. Beat until light and fluffy. Add eggs, beating well each time. Mix flour, baking powder and salt; add alternately with milk, beating well after each addition. Stir in vanilla. Bake at 350 degrees in a lightly greased tube pan for about one hour or until the cake springs back when you press on it gently with your fingers.

*A traditional pound cake uses a pound each of butter, sugar, flour, and eggs. This recipe uses about half a pound of each. The milk and baking powder make a lighter cake. Leave them out if you want a real, honest-to-goodness, old fashioned pound cake.

Nut Cake

2 cups flour
2 tsp. baking powder
½ tsp salt
2 cups pecans
2 cups sugar
1 cup butter
1 tsp. vanilla
8 eggs

Sift together 4 times: flour, baking powder, and salt. Cream the sugar and butter until smooth then add eggs and flour. Coat the pecans with flour before adding them to the batter so they won't sink to the bottom of the cake. Pour into 3 greased and floured small loaf pans and bake at 350 degrees for 45 - 60 minutes, until done.

Lila's Standby Applesauce-Date Cake

2 cups sugar
¾ cup shortening
2 eggs
2 cups flour
2 tsp baking powder
2 tsp baking soda
2 tsp. cinnamon
1 tsp. nutmeg
½ tsp. cloves
2 cups applesauce
2 cups pecans
8 oz. dates, chopped
1 cup raisins

Cream together shortening and sugar; add eggs. Sift in dry ingredients alternating with applesauce. Add dates, raisins, and pecans. Fill greased and floured loaf pans. Bake at 300 degrees for one hour, or until toothpick in center comes out clean.

K's Fruitcake

K made her fruitcake for years before she saw Lila's Applesauce-Date Cake recipe, but they are very similar. Follow directions in the recipe above with these changes:
Double the amount of cinnamon, nutmeg and cloves.
Add 1 quart fig preserves, 1 quart pear preserves, 1 quart watermelon rind preserves, and 1 quart mincemeat instead of the 2 cups applesauce. Double the amount of pecans, dates, and raisins. Add half a cup of candied orange peel. Add extra flour if needed, a little at a time, till batter is very moist but not runny. Fill greased and floured loaf pans. Decorate with candied cherries and pecan halves. Bake at 300 degrees for one hour, or until toothpick in center comes out clean. Wrap in a clean white cuptowel and store in a cool dark place for a week or two to improve flavor. The cloth allows the cake to breathe and not spoil.

Cookies

Four O'clock Honk

Aunt Lucile and K were in the middle of canning - hot, hard, heavy, hurried work - when a swarm of little children came running into the kitchen. "We're hungry! What can we eat?" Aunt Lucile in her loving voice laughed, "Everybody's coming in here all day long honking for something to eat. From now on, you can have a ten o'clock honk and a four o'clock honk. Otherwise, run outside and play till suppertime." But she handed each one a couple of cookies on their way out.

Forever after, when the clock struck four, we said, "Time for our Four O'clock Honk."

Oatmeal Cookies

1 cup shortening
2 cups sugar
2 eggs
½ cup buttermilk
1¾ cups flour
1 tsp. baking soda
1 tsp. baking powder
1 tsp. salt
1 tsp. cinnamon
1 tsp. nutmeg
3 cups oatmeal
1 tsp. vanilla
½ cup raisins
½ cup nuts

Cream shortening and sugar. Stir in eggs then milk. Sift together dry ingredients; stir them in, then add oats, nuts, and raisins. Drop spoonfuls on greased cookie sheet. Bake 400 degrees for about 8 minutes. Makes about 5 dozen cookies.

Molasses Oatmeal Cookies

1 ¼ cups sugar
½ cup butter
1/3 cup molasses
2 eggs
1 cup raisins
2 cups rolled oats
1 2/3 cups flour
¼ tsp salt
1 tsp. soda
1 tsp. cinnamon

In large bowl, stir together sugar, butter, molasses and eggs. Sift in dry ingredients, mix well. Stir in oats and raisins. Drop by rounded teaspoonfuls, 2 inches apart on ungreased cookie sheets. Bake 9 to 10 minutes at 375° just until set.

Sugar was rationed during World War Two. Many recipes used molasses or honey instead. Good thing we had lots of honey from Daddy's bees, and home-grown molasses!

Applesauce Oatmeal Cookies

½ cup butter
¾ cup molasses
1 egg
1 cup applesauce
2 cups oatmeal
1½ cups flour
2 tsp. baking powder
½ tsp. baking soda
½ tsp. salt
2 tsp. cinnamon

Mix butter, molasses, and egg. Sift dry ingredients together; add alternately with applesauce. Stir in oatmeal. Bake 350 degrees just till lightly browned.

----

*K had fun thinking up variations on a few basic recipes. She might: 1. Stir fruit preserves into different kinds of cookie dough. 2. Press ½ tsp. jam into top of cookies before baking. 3. Use homemade mincemeat instead of applesauce. 4. Add raisins or nuts. 5. Use cinnamon, nutmeg, allspice, cloves, or ginger in various combinations.

Chewy Molasses Cookies

1 large egg
½ cup butter
½ cup sugar
½ cup molasses
½ tsp salt
2 cups flour
2 tsp. soda
2 tsp. cinnamon
½ tsp. ginger
¼ tsp. cloves

Mix egg, butter, sugar, and molasses in a medium-sized bowl. Sift in dry ingredients; mix well. Make out into balls, roll in sugar. Bake 375° for 8-10 minutes until cookies are puffed, cracked, and just set around edges. Molasses keeps these cookies fresh and chewy. *For chewy cookies, bake just until set, not browned.

Butter Molasses Cookies

¾ cup molasses
½ cup butter
½ tsp. baking soda
2 ¼ cups flour
1 tsp. baking powder
1 tsp. cinnamon

Heat molasses to boiling. Remove from heat and stir in butter and soda. Add flour mixed with baking powder and cinnamon. Make out balls; press with fingers to flatten on cookie sheet. Bake at 350 degrees 5 or 6 minutes.
* If cookies get hard after a few days, put a slice of apple in the cookie tin to make them soft and chewy again.

Honey Ginger Cookies

¾ cup shortening, melted
1 cup sugar
¼ cup honey
1 egg
2 cups flour
2 tsp. ginger
½ tsp. cloves

Mix. Make 1 inch balls. Roll in sugar. Flatten in pan. Cook at 375 degrees just until set. *Try putting ½ tsp. preserves on top of each cookie before baking.

Honey Nut Cookies

1/3 cup butter
½ cup honey
1 egg
½ tsp vanilla
1¼ cup flour
½ tsp. soda
½ tsp. salt
½ cup nuts

Sift dry ingredients together. Mix everything together in order listed. Drop by spoonfuls on greased cookie sheet. Bake 375 degrees for 6 or 7 minutes.

Old Fashioned Tea Cakes

1 cup sugar
1 egg
½ cup butter
1 tsp. vanilla
3 cups flour
1 tsp. soda
½ tsp. salt
1 tsp. nutmeg

Mix first four, then add dry ingredients; make walnut sized balls. Press balls out with the bottom of a glass dipped in sugar. Bake at 375 degrees for 7 or 8 minutes.

Sugar Cookies

1½ cups sugar
1 cup butter
2 eggs
2¾ cups flour
1 tsp baking powder
1 tsp. vanilla

Cream sugar and butter, stir in eggs and vanilla. Add sifted dry ingredients; mix well. Drop onto greased cookie sheet. Bake at 375 degrees till brown around the edges.

Pecan Cookies

½ cup shortening
½ cup butter
2½ cups brown sugar
2 beaten eggs
2½ cups flour
¼ tsp. soda
¼ tsp. salt
1 cup chopped pecans

Sift dry ingredients together. Mix everything in order listed. Drop spoonfuls 2 inches apart on a greased cookie sheet. Bake 350 degrees 12 to 15 minutes.

----

*If you don't have brown sugar: one cup white sugar plus one Tbsp. molasses = one cup brown sugar.

Aunt Sabie's Sugar Crisps

¾ cup shortening
1 cup sugar
¼ c. molasses
1 egg
2 c. flour
½ tsp. salt
2 tsp. soda
½ tsp. cloves
½ tsp. ginger
1 tsp. cinnamon

Melt shortening over low heat. Let it cool. Stir in sugar, molasses, and egg. Sift and add dry ingredients, mix well. Chill about 2 hours. Form into little balls the size of a large marble and roll in sugar. Bake on greased cookie sheets 2 inches apart at 375 degrees for 8 to 10 minutes.

Aunt Lucile's Peanut Butter Cookies

1 cup shortening
1 cup white sugar
1 cup brown sugar
1 cup peanut butter
2 eggs
2½ cups flour
2 tsp. soda
½ tsp. salt

Cream shortening and sugars; add peanut butter and eggs. Sift dry ingredients together, stir in, mix well. Make balls of dough; put on cookie sheet; flatten twice with fork, this way then that way, to make a crisscross pattern on top. Bake 375 degrees for 8 to 10 minutes until lightly browned. Makes 5 dozen.

Lois said, "Aunt Lucile had a beautiful cookie tin, about a foot across and four inches tall, black with yellow roses all over the top. Every time we went to her house, the tin was <u>full</u> of Peanut Butter Cookies!"

Candy

Payday Candy

When K was a girl, her Mama bought groceries and put them "on account." Once a month, on payday, when Papa went in and paid the bill, the grocer gave him a sack full of hard candy. Papa divided the candy into little piles, one for each family member. What K got that day was her candy for the month. She ate it slowly, to make it last.

K loved candy, but she didn't make it often. It took so much sugar to make enough candy for such a large family! Something with flour in it would go farther. When she made Chocolate Fudge, Divinity, or Penuche, K's face was beaming, her whole manner rejoicing; she made it a special occasion. When we made Syrup Sticks, which is Molasses Taffy, we made a party out of it, even if only our family was there. We always had date loaf at Christmas.

Syrup Sticks

2 cups molasses	2 Tbsp. butter
2 cups sugar	2 Tbsp. vinegar

Cook everything together in a heavy boiler. Stir constantly till sugar is dissolved and mixture comes to a boil, then cook without stirring to hard ball stage. Pour candy out onto a buttered plate. Use the egg turner to turn the edges toward the center several times to help it cool off quicker, until the candy is cool enough to handle. Everybody butter your hands and get a lump of the candy; pull it out, double it up, and pull again until the candy turns a lighter color. K's always turned a beautiful amber, almost a golden color. Some of us never had much candy left by then because we kept taking bites out of the middle as we pulled it. K was having the best time! We had a kitchen full of children, laughing, clowning around, while pulling all that sticky candy! It was a celebration of the fun things in life, and the joyful memories have far outlived the mess.

Vinegar Taffy

3 cups sugar	1 cup water
½ cup vinegar	2 Tbsp. butter

Cook sugar, vinegar, and water over low heat to soft ball stage. Stir in butter. Pour onto a buttered plate until cool enough to handle. Butter your hands well before pulling. The more you pull, the whiter it gets.

Once when K and Daddy were gone somewhere, Lois mixed some cocoa and sugar together and put a pinch of it inside her lower lip. It was her snuff. Don't tell K.

Chocolate Fudge

3 cups sugar
2/3 cup cocoa
1/8 tsp. salt
1½ cups milk
¼ cup butter
1 tsp. vanilla

Mix sugar, cocoa powder, and salt; slowly add milk. Stir constantly till it comes to a boil then don't stir any more. Cook to soft ball stage. Remove from heat. Add butter and vanilla but do not stir until lukewarm. Beat until fudge thickens and loses its gloss. Pour into buttered dish. Cut into squares when cool.

Date Loaf

3 cups sugar
1 cup milk
½ lb. dates
2 cups chopped nuts

Mix sugar, milk, and dates in a medium boiler. Boil and stir over medium heat until it leaves pan when tilted (soft ball stage). Do not overcook. Stir in nuts; beat till slightly thick. Pour the candy out onto a wet flour sack cuptowel. Roll up, shaping candy into a log. Wrap the wet towel in a dry towel and let it set overnight. Slice thin.

Peanut Brittle

1 cup white corn syrup
1 cup sugar
2 cups raw peanuts
a pinch of salt
1 tsp. baking soda

Mix syrup, sugar, peanuts and salt. Bring to a boil and cook until color changes. Peanuts will pop open. Remove from heat. Add soda; stir until color changes. Pour onto buttered cookie sheet. Break in pieces when cool.

Penuche

2 cups sugar
1 cup light cream
2 Tbsp. butter
1 cup sugar
2 Tbsp. butter
2 cups nuts

Boil 2 cups sugar, l cup light cream, and 2 Tbsp. butter to soft ball stage. Remove from heat. In a different pan, cook one cup sugar and 2 Tbsp. butter until it caramelizes. Stir caramel into first mixture. Beat, adding chopped nuts, and continue beating until waxy. Spread in buttered pan. Cut in squares when firm.

Divinity Candy

2 ½ cups sugar
½ cup white corn syrup
½ cup water
2 egg whites
1 tsp. vanilla
1 cup nuts

In 2 quart pan, combine sugar, corn syrup, and water. Cook without stirring to soft ball stage. While syrup is cooking, beat egg whites to stiff peaks. Always beat egg whites in a grease-free bowl or pan. Gradually pour half of syrup over egg whites, beating constantly. Cook the other half of the syrup to hard crack stage. Beat into the egg white mixture. Add vanilla and nuts; beat till candy holds its shape, 4 or 5 minutes. Drop by large spoonfuls onto greased plate or cookie sheet.

----

*If you try to make Divinity Candy on a rainy or humid day, the candy will absorb moisture from the air and get sticky; it will not set up properly.

Puddin' & PIEs

Daddy's Birthday Pie

Daddy's birthday came toward the end of September, just as the sweet potatoes were getting ready. Daddy dug under a few plants with his hands. "There's a big one to the south," he smiled, "and another to the west." He pulled out the biggest ones. Soon he had enough to take to K so she could make him a birthday pie. He never wanted a cake; just the first Sweet Potato Pie of the season.

Sweet Potato Pie

2 cups sweet potatoes
½ cup butter
1 cup sugar
½ cup milk
3 eggs
½ tsp. nutmeg
2 tsp. cinnamon
1 unbaked pie crust

Boil 4 or 5 whole sweet potatoes for 45 to 50 minutes or bake at 350 degrees for l hour, until soft. Remove peels; mash and measure out 2 cups. Mix everything together; pour into unbaked pie crust. Bake at 350 degrees for about one hour until a knife inserted near the center comes out clean.

Pumpkin Pie

1½ cups cooked pumpkin
¾ cups sugar
3 eggs, slightly beaten
1 can evaporated milk
½ tsp. salt
2 tsp. cinnamon
1 tsp. ginger
½ tsp. nutmeg
¼ tsp. cloves
1 unbaked pie crust

Mix together pumpkin, sugar, salt, and spices. Stir in eggs and milk. This recipe fills one very deep dish pie crust, or two small ones. Bake at 400 degrees for 50 minutes, or till knife inserted near center comes out clean.

Mincemeat Pie

Make Green Tomato Mincemeat by recipe on page 65.
Make up enough pie crust for a double-crust pie. Pour one pint of mincemeat into bottom crust. Make lattice top crust: Cut strips ½ inch wide and 12 inches long. Lay strips on top of pie l inch apart. Fold back alternate strips to help you weave crosswise strips over and under till top is covered. Bake at 400 degrees for 35 to 40 minutes

Pie Crust made with Lard

1½ cups flour
½ tsp. salt
½ cup lard
3 or 4 Tbsp. cold water

K sifted the flour and salt together then worked in the lard with her fingers. She added cold water one spoonful at a time until the dough would hold together. Too much water makes a tough, hard crust, not flaky. K put a little flour on the breadboard and rolled out the crust.

For a **double crust** pie, use
2 cups flour, 2/3 cup lard, and 5 Tbsp. water.

Pie Crust made with Butter

2½ cups flour
½ tsp. salt
1 cup real butter
6 Tbsp. cold water

Sift together flour and salt. Work in half of butter till like coarse crumbs; cut in other half till the size of small peas. Sprinkle one tablespoon of cold water into flour mixture at a time, stirring each time. Keep stirring until dough holds together. If dough crumbles or has dry spots, add just a little bit more water; too much water will make the crust hard and tough. Keep stirring until you can make a ball. Divide in half. Roll out crusts. Makes crust for two pies, or top and bottom for a two-crust pie.

K baked the scraps and pieces of crust that she trimmed off around the edge of the pie pan. It was good to nibble on. She called it **Crust Food**.

Peach Pie

K always cooked her peach pie in the biscuit pan; it was a 9x13 aluminum pan that showed much wear and spoke of many special meals (which was her way of showing love) with pie or bread pudding or buttered biscuits. She mixed a double batch of pie crust with quick, practiced strokes, shaped it into two flattened balls, and started rolling it out on her nice big bread board. K got a lot done, and didn't waste much time doing it. She patted the bottom crust into the rectangular pan, working it down into the corners and up over the sides.

K opened a jar of home-canned peaches, prying the sealed lid off with a spoon, and poured the peaches, juice and all into the bottom crust. A cup of sugar, maybe mixed with a little flour, sprinkled and stirred in a little bit, a few dabs of butter dotted here and there, and the pie was ready for the top crust. She quickly sealed the edges, trimmed off the scraps to be cooked as crust food, cut a few slits in the top, and slipped it in the oven (375?) to bake till it was golden brown and bubbly.

When we walked into the house, it smelled so good, we could hardly stand it. Smiling real big, Daddy sniffed the air and quipped, "Well it looks like we're going to have peach pie in about a week!" But right away, with excitement shining in her eyes, K sang out, "We're having Beach Bie!" That was *her* little joke, a quote from some small child, and we laughed with her.

Apple, Pear, and Blackberry pies were good, too; just open one of those many jars of canned fruit.

K's Chocolate Pie

1 ¼ cups sugar	3 egg yolks
½ cup flour	dash of salt
3 tablespoons cocoa	¼ cup butter
2 cups milk	1 tsp vanilla

Sift together all the dry ingredients. Add just enough milk to make a paste. Slowly stir in the rest of the milk, egg yolks, and salt. Cook over medium heat STIR CONSTANTLY. Mixture will begin to thicken and will try to stick to the bottom of the pan, don't let it. Remove from heat when mixture is like a thick pudding. Beat in butter and vanilla. Use a mixer to get out any lumps. Pour into a deep dish pre-baked pie crust. Top with Meringue.

Meringue

3 egg whites	½ tsp. vanilla
¼ tsp. cream of tartar	6 Tbsp. sugar

Start with a grease-free bowl and utensils. Blend egg whites and cream of tartar. Add vanilla. Beat until the eggs hold a peak. Slowly add the sugar. Beat until the sugar isn't grainy. Spread over the pie being careful to seal in the edges. Touch lightly to make peaks. Brown at 350F.

Note: Utensils must be totally grease-free.
Note: Meringue may bead or pull away from sides if cooled too quickly.

Green Grape Pie

K enjoyed **Green Grape Pie** and **Vinegar Pie** *because* they were so sour; she shivered at the thought of how sour they were. When Lila, Lois, Margaret, Ben and I tried to recall a recipe, we all agreed the pies were *too* sour. From there on, our memories are somewhat different.

Lila remembers, "The grapes were picked immature, before the seeds got hard. We always picked wild grapes. K canned jars of whole grapes with their juice. Whether she used fresh or canned grapes for her pie, they were cooked down soft. She put the grapes and the liquid they were cooked in, a good bit of sugar, and probably some flour; cooked the filling till it got thick, and poured it into a baked crust."

Lois remembers, "Daddy grew concord grapes. They didn't all get ripe at once. In the same cluster, most were fully ripe, but many were still green. Daddy picked them all. It was our job to separate them out. K canned jars of purple grape juice to make into jelly during the winter when the stove's heat would be welcome. She canned green grape juice for Green Grape Pie. We didn't know anybody else who made it; it was K's own recipe. She put eggs, sugar, flour, and the green grape juice; cooked a smooth filling in a boiler on top of the stove and poured it into the baked pie shell. It was like a cream pie recipe."

Saralou remembers, "My memory of Green Grape Pie is in those two little spots under my throat that kinda grinch when I think about how sour it was."

Margaret remembers, "I think it was white."

Ben remembers, "As I recall, the Green Grape Pie and Vinegar Pie were very similar, in that they were essentially juice, sweetened with a lot of sugar and thickened with flour, baked in a regular crust with additional crust pieces acting rather like dumplings. Bake the crust brown, scoop out crust and thick juice, and eat it if you can. The Green Grape was too tart and Vinegar too sour for my taste." We all agree that Vinegar Pie had dumplings. The dumplings may have been pie crust or some other dough. I don't know how much vinegar she used.

K made Green Grape Pie over a period of fifty years. Likely, she cooked it all the different ways we remember. Here is a probable recipe using K's basic cream pie recipe, page 106, but substituting green grape juice for the milk.

Green Grape Pie

2 cups green grape
1½ cups sugar
½ cup flour
2 eggs
¼ cup butter
1 baked pie crust

Use 2 cups cooked green grapes with juice, <u>or</u> use 2 cups of green grape juice. Mix sugar and flour together. Add just enough juice to make a paste. Slowly stir in remaining grapes and/or juice. Cook and stir over medium-high heat till bubbly; then cook and stir for two minutes. Remove from heat. Stir a good bit of the hot mixture into the eggs, then stir it all back into the filling in the pan; cook till thick like pudding, stirring constantly. Add butter, beat well. Pour into baked pie crust.

Basic Cream Pie

1 cup sugar
½ cup flour
dash of salt
2 cups milk
3 egg yolks
¼ cup butter
1 tsp. vanilla
1 baked pie crust

Mix sugar, flour, and salt together. Gradually stir in milk. Cook and stir over medium-high heat till bubbly. Cook and stir 2 minutes. Remove from heat. Stir a good bit of the hot mixture into the egg yolks then stir it all back into the filling in the pan; cook till thick, stirring constantly. Beat in butter and vanilla. Pour into baked pie crust.
*Variations: 1. Add a cup of Coconut 2. Add sliced Bananas 3. Decrease milk to 1 cup. Add one can crushed Pineapple with juice (about 2½ cups) before cooking the filling.
4. Make up one you like. Use Meringue recipe page 103.

Lemon Meringue Pie

1 ½ cups sugar
½ cup flour
Dash of salt
1 ½ cups hot water
3 egg yolks
2 Tbsp. butter
juice of 2 lemons
1 baked pie crust

Mix sugar, flour, and salt in a middle-sized boiler. Slowly pour in hot water, stirring constantly. Cook and stir till mixture boils. Turn heat down; cook 8 minutes over low heat, stirring constantly. Remove from heat. Stir some of the hot mixture into the egg yolks then stir egg yolks into the filling in the pan. Return to boiling and cook 4 minutes, stirring constantly. Beat in butter; slowly add lemon juice; mix well. Pour into baked pie crust. Use Meringue recipe, page 103. Brown at 350 degrees for 12 to 15 minutes.

Buttermilk Pie

½ cup butter
2 cups sugar
3 eggs
2 rounded Tbsp. flour
dash of nutmeg
1 cup buttermilk
1 tsp. vanilla
9 inch pie crust

Mix ingredients in order listed. Pour into a 9 inch unbaked pie crust. Bake at 350 degrees for 45 minutes or till knife in center comes out clean.

Chess Pie

1 cup sugar
¼ cup butter
4 eggs
1 Tbsp. vinegar
1 Tbsp. cornmeal
1 Tbsp. flour
1 tsp. vanilla
unbaked pie crust

Cream sugar and butter; add other ingredients one at a time, mixing well after each addition. Pour into the pie crust. Bake at 350°F for 25 to 35 minutes or until golden brown and the center is set; it may wiggle a little if you shake the pie gently.

Buttermilk Chess Pie

1½ cups sugar
2 Tbsp. cornmeal
2 Tbsp. flour
Pinch of salt
½ cup butter
½ cup buttermilk
2 tsp. vanilla
4 large eggs
juice of one lemon
unbaked pie crust

Mix ingredients in order listed. Pour into pie crust and bake at 350 degrees for 30 to 35 minutes, until golden brown and set.

Custard Pie

4 eggs
½ cup sugar
¼ tsp. salt
½ tsp. vanilla
2 ½ cups milk
1 unbaked pie crust

Mix eggs, sugar, salt, and vanilla. Scald milk; gradually stir in. Pour into unbaked pie crust. Sprinkle with nutmeg. Bake in 350 degree oven 35 to 40 minutes, or till knife in center comes out clean.

Bread Pudding

2 cups milk
2 eggs
2 cups bread crumbs
½ cup sugar
3 Tbsp. butter
1 tsp. cinnamon
1 tsp. vanilla
¼ tsp. salt
½ cup raisins
Sprinkle of nutmeg

K saved up the leftover biscuits and lightbread to make bread pudding with. Mix the milk and eggs in a bowl. Crumble the bread and stir it in. Let it soak a while, then stir in remaining ingredients. Butter a baking pan and pour everything into it. Sprinkle a little nutmeg on top. Bake at 350 degrees about 45 minutes to an hour, till a knife comes out clean. The outside gets a little bit crusty, but the inside is like pudding, not dry.

Homemade Chocolate Sauce for Bread Pudding

1 cup sugar
¼ cup cocoa
½ cup of milk
a spoonful of butter

Boil and stir till the sugar isn't grainy and the sauce thickens. Pour on top of the bread pudding.

Vanilla Pudding

2 Tbsp. flour	2 cups milk	2 tsp. vanilla
½ cup sugar	2 eggs	1 Tbsp. butter
¼ tsp. salt		

Mix sugar, flour and salt; add just enough milk to make a paste. Slowly stir in the rest of the milk and the eggs. Cook until thick, stirring constantly. Remove from heat and stir in vanilla and butter. Pour into serving dishes.

Chocolate Pudding - increase sugar to 1 cup. Add 2 Tbsp. cocoa and mix it with the sugar and flour. Cook as above.

Banana Pudding

Cook vanilla pudding, recipe above. Butter the biscuit pan. Put a layer of vanilla wafers covering bottom and sides. Slice a layer of bananas on top of the vanilla wafers. Pour 1/3 of pudding over bananas and wafers. Keep putting layers of vanilla wafers, bananas, and pudding till dish is full, ending with vanilla wafers on top. K doubled the vanilla pudding recipe. Banana Pudding was G's favorite.

----

*Put the banana peels around the base of your rose bushes; they're a natural rose fertilizer.

Rice and Raisins

2 cups water	½ cup raisins	sugar
1 cup rice	butter	milk

K cooked the rice and raisins together until the rice was done and the raisins soft. When we got our bowlful we stirred in some milk, butter, and sugar. Sprinkled in a little cinnamon if we had it.

God Leads His Dear Children Along

K and Daddy led their dear children along some good paths. They gave us: Love of God, country, and family; respect for sacred things, for self, and for others; curious, inquisitive minds and a quest for learning; a love of words and reading; enjoyment of working the soil and watching things grow; and a love of music and singing. Daddy enjoyed singing this song.

God Leads Us Along

In shady, green pastures,
so rich and so sweet,
God leads His dear children along;
Where the water's cool flow
bathes the weary one's feet,
God leads His dear children along.

Some through the waters, some through the flood,
Some through the fire, but all through the blood;
Some through great sorrow, but God gives a song,
In the night seasons and all the day long.

Jesus said, "I am the good shepherd; the good shepherd gives His life for the sheep."
His sheep know His voice, and they follow Him.
John 10

Afterword

K's Kitchen serves up a slice of life as our family lived it growing up in the '30s, and '40s. We lived in several little country communities scattered across rural East Texas where Daddy taught in little two-room country schools and preached in little half-time country churches. We were a close-knit family and still are.

K cooked for a big family. She most likely would have doubled or tripled the recipes as I have them in this book. Only K didn't cook by a recipe. She didn't measure. Like most country cooks of her generation, she knew the look and feel of what was right for whatever she was fixing. Once Margaret asked how much flour to put in something; K cupped one hand and said, "about this much." Cooking was more an art than a science, and a recipe was a guideline to be altered according to personal taste and ingredients on hand. K had quite a few basic "recipes" in her mind, and she enjoyed making up variations of them, just to have something different.

In 1949 we moved to town. Life became more modern, more scientific. Cookbooks, magazines, and the recipe section of the newspaper slowly changed our thinking. K would look at a recipe and say, "That looks like the way I cook it, only I don't put this and I add that." Later when we girls got grown with families of our own to cook for, we started asking K for her recipes of our childhood favorites. We have a few written down exactly the way she told them. K's Chocolate Pie on page 103 is one. Margaret wrote home for K's Dressing recipe and K's reply is a classic. You can see it on page 52. I called and got her recipe for Date Loaf. We found a lot of recipes in her handwriting in her recipe box; the box lid said Assorted Greeting Cards. When I asked how to make fruitcake, Lila dug out her recipe for Applesauce-Date Cake and showed it to us. K said, "Yes, I make my fruitcake like this, only I put in the jars of preserves, and you'll need a little extra flour to take up the juice from the preserves." So gradually we made a collection of K's recipes which we share with you here.

Thank you, Lila, Lois, Margaret, and Ben for sharing recipes and memories. Lately Lila and Lois have spent many hours on the phone helping me remember how it was in the old days. I'm glad Daddy, K, and G wrote out their memories before they passed away. Mat didn't need to write anything; nobody could ever forget him and the part he played in our lives.

Thanks to my husband, Paul, for being such a willing taster in my "test kitchen," especially when tasting cookies, pies, and bread pudding.

Lois drew the pictures on the cover and in the book, except I did that little sign on page 39.

Lila said I could put this next piece in the book; she wrote it when Lois and her children brought K a present. One of the children said, "We brought you a surprise; it's a shiny new stove!"

So here it is, "Final Thoughts of the Old Stove Upon Retirement and Replacement."

Final Thoughts of the Old Stove Upon Retirement and Replacement

By Lila

I can't understand, myself, why they're all standing around shedding tears. Human beings are peculiar people; they say they like changes, but they don't. Now take a look at me, I say, take an honest look. I've got a door like an alarm clock, a thermostat that's less than safe, and one burner that, far as I remember, has never been lit. Now look at the Boss Lady here. She and I have kept each other hot and kept each other going all these years. All those biscuits. All that bacon and gravy. Do you have any idea how many hot rolls, and pound cakes and buttermilk pies we've turned out, right here in this kitchen? Holidays were the worst. "Nice holiday!" everybody said - "Humph!" said the dishpan to me, and me to it. We chewed it over plenty after they left out. Well it wasn't that bad. Any good stove you could name would feel proud of a nice brown turkey, and K's fruit cake. Well, all of it, really, from water for one cup of coffee (boiling away!) to the biggest boiler full of blackberry jelly. It's like a person who raised a lot of children; she won't remember the day on the calendar she made pecan cookies, or the date she made peach pie; it's a general memory of warmth and aroma. These people here, they'll keep on with all that, but I'm give out and I give up. I'm going out and rest myself. Now hear what they're saying: But the Replacement won't be the same! Of course it won't. It'll have a thermostat you can count on and burners that all of them light.

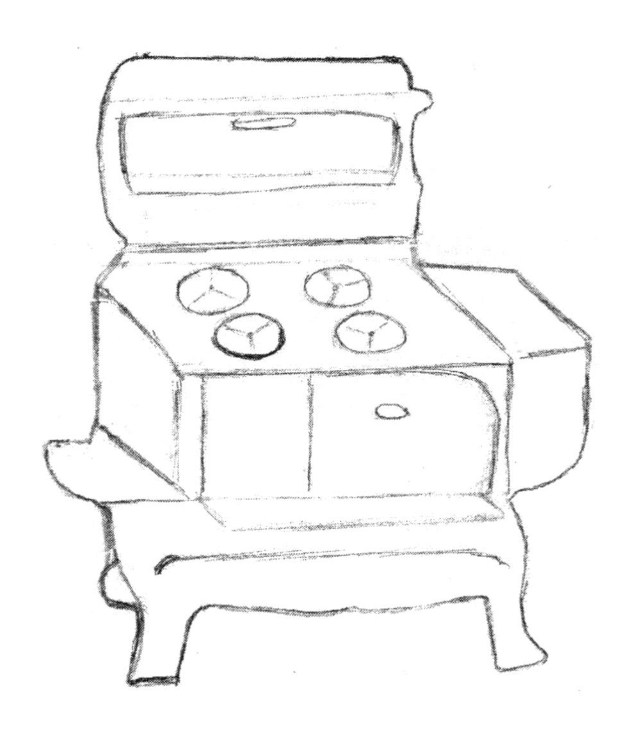

DATE DUE

PRINTED IN U.S.A.

Made in the USA
Lexington, KY
11 March 2019